Portfolio and Performance Assessment in Teacher Education

Related Titles of Interest

Successful College Teaching: Problem-Solving Strategies of Distinguished Professors
Sharon A. Baiocco and Jamie N. DeWaters
ISBN: 0-205-26654-1

Colleges and Universities as Citizens
Robert G. Bringle, Richard Games, and Reverend Edward A. Malloy, CSC
ISBN: 0-205-28696-8

Faculty Work and Public Trust: Restoring the Value of Teaching and Public Service in American Academic Life
James S. Fairweather
ISBN: 0-205-17948-7

Emblems of Quality in Higher Education: Developing and Sustaining High-Quality Programs
Jennifer Grant Haworth and Clifton F. Conrad
ISBN: 0-205-19546-6

Writing for Professional Publication: Keys to Academic and Business Success
Kenneth T. Henson
ISBN: 0-205-28313-6

Revitalizing General Education in a Time of Scarcity: A Navigational Chart for Administrators and Faculty
Sandra L. Kanter, Zelda F. Gamson, and Howard B. London
ISBN: 0-205-26257-0

The Adjunct Professor's Guide to Success: Surviving and Thriving in the College Classroom
Richard E. Lyons, Marcella L. Kysilka, and George E. Pawlas
ISBN: 0-205-28774-3

Multicultural Course Transformation in Higher Education: A Broader Truth
Ann Intili Morey and Margie K. Kitano (Editors)
ISBN: 0-205-16068-9

Sexual Harassment on Campus: A Guide for Administrators, Faculty, and Students
Bernice R. Sandler and Robert J. Shoop
ISBN: 0-205-16712-8

Designing and Teaching an On-Line Course: Spinning Your Web Classroom
Heidi Schweizer
ISBN: 0-205-30321-8

Leadership in Continuing and Distance Education in Higher Education
Cynthia C. Jones Shoemaker
ISBN: 0-205-26823-4

Shaping the College Curriculum: Academic Plans in Action
Joan S. Stark and Lisa R. Lattuca
ISBN: 0-205-16706-3

For more information or to purchase a book, please call 1-800-278-3525.

Portfolio and Performance Assessment in Teacher Education

Dorothy M. Campbell
Beverly J. Melenyzer
Diane H. Nettles
Richard M. Wyman, Jr.

California University of Pennsylvania

Allyn and Bacon

Boston • London • Toronto • Sydney • Tokyo • Singapore

Executive Editor & Publisher: Stephen D. Dragin
Series Editorial Assistant: Bridget McSweeney
Marketing Manager: Brad Parkins
Manufacturing Buyer: David Repetto

Copyright © 2000 by Allyn & Bacon
A Pearson Education Company
Needham Heights, MA 02494

Internet: www.abacon.com

Library of Congress Cataloging-in-Publication Data

Portfolio and performance assessment in teacher education / Dorothy M.
    Campbell . . . [et al.].
        p.   cm.
    Includes bibliographical references (p.   ) and index.
    ISBN 0-205-30850-3
    1. Portfolios in education.   2. Teachers—Rating of.   3. Teachers—
Training of.   I. Campbell, Dorothy M.
LB1728.P667   2000
370'.71'55—dc21   99-23805
                                                                        CIP

Printed in the United States of America

10   9   8   7   6   5   4   3   2   1   03   02   01   00   99

Contents

▶

Preface

The intended audience for this book is the host of teacher educators who are interested in utilizing professional portfolios with the teachers they are preparing. A professional portfolio is widely advocated as an effective marketing tool for prospective teachers in that it provides tangible evidence of what the candidate can do in practice. Beyond this limited benefit, however, portfolios are valued by many teacher education programs that implement a performance-based assessment system. Such a system holds learners accountable for demonstrating achievement of complex tasks required to fulfill the role of teacher. Teacher educators who are attracted to portfolios because they are an effective vehicle for movement toward more authentic, broad-based assessment of actual teacher performance, as well as assessment of program quality, encounter many challenges and many pressures for change. If you are in this category, you are realizing that portfolios designed to assess teaching performance are not a comfortable "add-on" to your existing program.

Genuine assessment of performance inevitably changes the way candidates learn and the way programs in teacher education do business. It is no longer enough to march students through a sequence of courses with the outcome being a grade point average and a score on a certification examination. Instead, teacher educators must assume responsibility for enabling students to perform as competent teachers and for documenting this achievement.

We have written this book for faculty who are challenged by this larger perspective of portfolio use. We set forth elements we found to be important as we designed a performance-based portfolio assessment system in our teacher education program. These four critical elements of a portfolio assessment system are: (1) establishing and communicating the program parameters of philosophy, standards, and portfolio requirements; (2) monitoring the quality in student learning through course-embedded performance assessments and rubrics; (3) supporting students as they document their learning through strategies such as mentoring, work in partnership schools, and checkpoints; and (4) developing a comprehensive plan for assessment of candidates and the teacher education program.

The first requirement of a portfolio assessment system is having a clear vision of what the teacher education program views as competent professional performance. In Chapter 1, we put forth the notion that you can effectively communicate this vision of competence through a philosophy of teaching and learning and through the adoption of a set of professional standards. The philosophy and standards become the real focus of all faculty and student effort. The portfolio is a powerful and effective vehicle for maintaining this focus.

Once a philosophy and a set of standards have been developed, you need to create opportunities for students to achieve and document the standards. Students will need a set of guidelines on how to develop portfolios that document growth in achieving standards within a philosophical context. Students will need to understand the goals of your program and the rationale for portfolio work as well as the practical aspects of portfolio organization. Guidelines should also address all requirements for portfolios that are unique to your particular program. In Chapter 2 we discuss the possible content for program guidelines for portfolio development.

After defining a philosophy, a set of standards, and guidelines for constructing portfolios, you may be tempted to perceive the logical next step to be planning a major culminating assessment of the standards with a portfolio presentation, defense, and evaluation. Putting all the assessment at the end of the program, however, puts enormous pressure on the teacher candidates and on the portfolio evaluators. Such an approach might actually pit candidates against the faculty who are teaching them and who would likely be among the evaluators. More importantly, ongoing opportunities for feedback and refinement of skills would be lost. Therefore, we contend that a much more effective approach is to share responsibility for the ongoing development of performance and assessment of standards with all faculty throughout the entirety of the students' preparation program. One way to do this is to move students toward demonstrable performance of some aspect of one or more standards in every course taught and every experience provided. Teacher educators have always attempted to design course content that develops understandings, skills, and dispositions necessary for effective teaching. The new challenge for faculty is to find ways to make those understandings, skills, and dispositions visible in contexts that are faithful to real-life teaching. What are necessary are performance assessment tasks or projects that are tied to the adopted standards and require students to do something authentic with what they are learning. A second way to assess performance throughout a teacher education program is to design a series of portfolio rubrics to be applied at various points in a student's academic career. Chapter 3 discusses the challenge of maintaining high-quality learning through designing engaging, valid, and authentic performance assessments for every course taught in the teacher education program and through the use of portfolio rubrics.

Students learning to be teachers need even more than a guiding philosophy, clear standards, performance assessments, and portfolio guidelines. They need ongoing personal support in their portfolio work so that they can effectively document their growth and take increasing control of their professional development. When students are left alone to do portfolio work, they tend to focus on organizing and justifying documentation of what they have already done well. It takes encounters with peers, faculty facilitators, and members of the larger professional community to challenge progress toward growing and changing, setting new goals, and designing new strategies for professional development. We contend that the more collaborative portfolio work becomes, the greater the growth in meeting the standards. This enabling approach to portfolio work is set forth in Chapter 4, in which we explore how a support system can operate throughout a student's entire program.

In Chapter 5, you will be reminded that every teacher education program needs a master plan for candidate and program assessment. More and more, judgment of overall program quality is being based on candidate performance. Thus, the guiding questions for program evaluation become: (1) What do our students know and what can they do when they graduate? (2) How will we assess the extent to which our students have attained the standards that we adopted? (3) What is the overall quality of our program as evidenced by student performance? (4) What type of evidence will we offer to indicate quality?

In Chapter 6, we review the process that we undertook as we implemented our portfolio system. In doing so, we explore the goals that we still need to meet and the ways that we met our tougher challenges. This gives you a complete picture of the assessment system that we use and the ways in which we are still learning as we go.

We have found that as students progress through a teacher education program that has a portfolio assessment system, they increasingly understand the power and potential of portfolios for giving direction to reflect on throughout their professional lives. Preservice teachers achieve a generalized understanding of how portfolios can be vehicles for managing their own professional development, for selling to others their professional competence in a compelling way, and for making visible the achievements of the students that they teach. If our students believe that portfolio work ends at an exit interview within their university or with a job offer, to a certain extent we have failed. It is essential that teacher candidates learn how portfolios can open horizons for ongoing teacher research, professional problem solving, and ever increasing competence.

The program described on these pages is the Elementary/Early Childhood Education Department housed within the College of Education and Human Service Professions at California University of Pennsylvania. The university is one of fourteen institutions governed by the Commonwealth of Pennsylvania's State System of Higher

Education. Located approximately 30 miles south of Pittsburgh, Pennsylvania, the university draws most of its 5,500 students from the region's mixture of rural and industrial communities. Approximately 750 undergraduate and 250 graduate students are enrolled in the Elementary/Early Childhood Education Program. The sixteen full-time and five adjunct faculty in Elementary/Early Childhood Education have embraced the goal of providing excellent preservice teacher education through performance and portfolio assessment.

A major component of our teaching and learning context is the Professional Development School (PDS) located at the Charleroi Area School District. We recognize the importance of providing settings in which our students can connect what they learn in the college class with their experiences in the school. The PDS site, located 10 miles from the university, is on a campus that includes an elementary center, a middle school, and a high school. The Charleroi Elementary Center is a K–5 facility with additional programs for students with special needs. The center houses thirty-three staff members and approximately six hundred students.

We offer this model as one way of addressing what we contend to be critical elements of teacher education programs with a portfolio and performance assessment system. Your program will need to find ways to establish program parameters, monitor quality of learning, support students as they refine performance, and develop a comprehensive plan for candidate and program evaluation. Every program will surely construct a unique approach to each of these elements. However, we share our story with the intention of suggesting new possibilities and clarifying what will likely be decision points for you.

Acknowledgments

Many individuals have contributed to the success of the portfolio assessment system described in this book. Perhaps the most helpful has been Karen Posa, our department secretary, who has worked with the portfolio program since its inception. Her organizational skills helped turn an unwieldy process into one that now, though still imperfect, operates far more efficiently. After viewing the process and benefits of portfolio development, Karen constructed a portfolio of her own. She says, "My portfolio has given me the opportunity to organize my accomplishments and identify my strengths." Karen's strengths are many. She has been a lifesaver to all those involved in this process. The authors of this book wish to express their gratitude and appreciation to Karen Posa for her tireless support and assistance in this undertaking.

We would also like to thank the students in the Elementary/ Early Childhood Education Department at California University. Our portfolio program was created for one and only one reason— because the faculty in our department believed that it would enhance the preparation of our students. Through the creation and delivery of the portfolio program our students have been a constant source of feedback. Their support and constructive criticism have contributed to both the success of the program and our belief in the value of student portfolios.

We would like to thank the following reviewers for their comments on the manuscript: Frances L. Clark, Wichita State University; Ruth Sower, Holy Family College; Courtney Moffatt, Edgewood College; Horace Rockwook, California University of PA; Mary Ann Battaglia, Peters Township School District; John Criswell, Edinboro University of PA; Caryn Pugliese, Slippery Rock University of PA; Judith Werner, Slippery Rock University of PA; Hilda Rosselli, University of South Florida; and Judith Wilkerson, University of South Florida.

Portfolio and Performance Assessment in Teacher Education

► 1

Gaining and Communicating a Vision

CHANGING EXPECTATIONS FOR TEACHERS

The most important factor in achieving quality student learning is the competence of the teacher (National Commission on Teaching and America's Future, 1996). To be a teacher a hundred years ago, one had to be considered a moral person with some degree of literacy. In the twentieth century the requirements for becoming a teacher have gradually gone beyond having good moral character and a nurturing personality to being an educated person with specialized training (Arends, 1994). Because of the complexities of our times, and because of the importance of teacher performance, America is again significantly redefining the qualifications for its teachers.

Teaching today is a profession that requires a high level of competency and a solid understanding of our society, child development, pedagogy, technology, and the subjects to be taught. Standards, which can be defined as expected learning outcomes that delineate the key aspects of the professional teaching role, must be met. To a large degree, it is teacher education programs that must meet the challenge of defining excellence and setting standards of professional competence that will meet the needs of education in the next century.

Calls for upgrading standards for American teachers and teacher education programs have been issued in this decade by numerous individuals and groups, including the National Commission on Teaching and America's Future (1996), a blue-ribbon group of twenty-six public officials and business and education leaders. These discussions challenge all teacher education programs to consider the question: What might we do to guarantee that our program provides top-notch training?

The starting point for an excellent teacher education program is clarity about the end product. A critical goal for any worthwhile teacher education program is consensus on a clear vision of the kind of teachers it wants to produce. Therefore, as a faculty interested in striving for a teacher education program that emphasizes performance, you will need to set standards that clarify what a graduating preservice teacher must know and be able to do. Additionally, your faculty must seek consensus on a set of assumptions about learning and teaching. A program that has set standards for the teachers it trains and has embedded those goals in a consistent philosophical orientation has a center from which to plan and revise curriculum, set priorities, and establish evaluation procedures. A well-articulated vision enables a teacher education program to be more than a collection of courses and experiences (Diez & Hass, 1997); it can become an integrated system that has identity and purpose. Moreover, a clear vision makes program self-evaluation possible. When you have collaborated on a set of standards and a philosophy statement, you can more easily detect redundancies, inconsistencies, and serious omissions in your program. Needed changes become obvious.

THE VISION: A FOCUS ON PRODUCT

A Philosophy of Teaching and Learning

Many organizations, educational and otherwise, have clarified goals, mission statements, and even philosophies that have not had a lasting or profound impact on their programs. In order to make a true difference, there must be ongoing study and refinement of the philosophy of the teacher education program. Our faculty is united around a constructivist philosophy, which we first articulated in writing for our own benefit in 1992.

Your philosophy will be meaningful when your faculty as a whole becomes involved in studying and discussing the program assumptions about learning and teaching. This is achieved as research articles are shared, observations are discussed, and clarifications are made. As understandings mature and the reading list grows, an individual or group from your faculty should be assigned to periodically ensure that these new understandings are reflected in the published philosophy document of the teacher education program.

Standards for Teachers

Many sets of standards for teachers are available today. This makes the job of teacher educators much easier. An existing set of standards may express well the expected outcomes for a particular program and therefore might be adopted by the program. Some teacher education programs as well as state departments of education are adopting INTASC standards, principles posited in September 1992 by the Interstate New Teacher Assessment and Support Consortium (Darling-Hammond, 1992). These standards were set for beginning teachers and have general applicability for teachers of all disciplines and grade levels. Some states have set their own standards. For example, the California Department of Education (1997) and the California Commission on Teacher Credentialing have collaborated on a set of standards for a formative portfolio assessment system of beginning teachers. The National Board for Professional Teaching Standards (1991) has established rigorous standards in several specific areas of teaching for certifying accomplished teachers.

However, it is important not to rush to adopt one of these sets of standards. It is necessary to have a sense of ownership of the standards used in your teacher education program, through faculty discussion and analysis. A technique for understanding the current priorities of your program is to sort all the objectives from your courses into groups of like objectives. These clusters can be given labels like "assessment" or "planning skills." The clusters can be compared to standards set by other groups and may reveal elements important to your particular institution. You may determine that you are more comfortable with your own standards or with an adapted version of another set. Through such an analytical process we generated an adapted version of the INTASC standards. Figure 1.1 explains the adaptations we made to the INTASC standards. Your program will no doubt have other priorities important to your vision of competent teaching.

FIGURE 1.1   Adaptations of INTASC Standards for Teaching Developed by California University of Pennsylvania Elementary/Early Childhood Education Faculty

---

The standards below were developed by Interstate New Teacher Assessment and Support Consortium (INTASC). Following each standard is the adaptation that the Elementary/Early Childhood Education Department at California University of Pennsylvania (CUP) has made. Differences in vernacular are italicized. Designated headings are also ours. An explanation is given for each change made by CUP.

Knowledge of Subject Matter

(INTASC) Standard #1: The teacher understands the central concepts, tools of inquiry, and structures of the discipline(s) he or she teaches and can create learning experiences that make these aspects of subject matter meaningful for students.

CUP: The teacher understands the central concepts, tools of inquiry, and structures of the disciplines *taught at the Elementary/Early Childhood levels.*

Explanation: Because other standards focus directly on providing learning experiences, our faculty members wanted this standard to have a clear single focus on subject matter knowledge. Thus, we shortened the statement and specified disciplines relevant to the Elementary/Early Childhood levels.

Knowledge of Human Development and Learning

(INTASC) Standard #2: The teacher understands how children learn and develop, and can provide learning opportunities that support their intellectual, social, and personal development.

CUP: Same

FIGURE 1.1 *Continued*

Adapting Instruction for Individual Needs

(INTASC) Standard #3: The teacher understands how students differ in their approaches to learning and creates instructional opportunities that are adapted to diverse learners.

CUP: Same

Multiple Instructional Strategies

(INTASC) Standard #4: The teacher understands and uses a variety of instructional strategies to encourage students' development of critical-thinking, problem-solving, and performance skills.

CUP: The teacher understands and uses a variety of instructional strategies that *integrate affective and cognitive objectives* and encourage students' development of critical-thinking, problem-solving, and performance skills.

Explanation: It is our view that all areas of development interact and affect each other. We consider affective development to be as important to address as cognitive development in the education of children. However, without a conscious awareness and effort the affective domain is often neglected. We chose to highlight this needed integration in this standard.

Classroom Motivation and Management Skills

(INTASC) Standard #5: The teacher uses an understanding of individual and group motivation and behavior to create a learning environment that encourages positive social interaction, active engagement in learning, and self-motivation.

CUP: Same

Communication Skills

(INTASC) Standard #6: The teacher uses knowledge of effective verbal, nonverbal, and media communication techniques to foster active inquiry, collaboration, and supportive interaction in the classroom.

CUP: The teacher uses knowledge of effective verbal, nonverbal, and media communication techniques *and utilizes appropriate and challenging classroom environments and materials* to foster active inquiry, collaboration, and supportive interaction in the classroom.

Explanation: Just as verbal and nonverbal behavior communicate powerfully in a classroom, so do media techniques, classroom environments, and teaching materials. We felt that it was important to emphasize the impact of physical environment and creative teaching materials as potentially effective communicators of classroom goals, expectations, and philosophy.

Instructional Planning Skills

(INTASC) Standard #7: The teacher plans instruction based upon knowledge of subject matter, students, the community, and curriculum goals.

Continued

FIGURE 1.1 *Continued*

CUP: The teacher plans instruction based upon knowledge of subject matter, students, the community, and curriculum goals *within his/her chosen philosophical orientation.*

Explanation: We contend that teachers plan most effectively when their planning is characterized by theoretical cohesiveness. Different philosophies make different assumptions about how curriculum should be organized. Therefore, teachers must be clear on the philosophical orientation that guides their planning and goal setting. We felt that our standard should reflect this.

Assessment of Student Learning

(INTASC) Standard #8: The teacher understands and uses formal and informal assessment strategies to ensure the continuous intellectual, social, and physical development of the learner.

CUP: Same

Professional Commitment and Responsibility

(INTASC) Standard #9: The teacher is a reflective practitioner who continually evaluates the effects of his/her choices and actions on others (students, parents, and other professionals in the learning community) and who actively seeks out opportunities to grow professionally.

CUP: Same

Partnerships

(INTASC) Standard #10: The teacher fosters relationships with school colleagues, parents, and agencies in the larger community to support students' learning and well-being.

CUP: The teacher fosters relationships with school colleagues, parents, agencies, *and cultural organizations* in the larger community to support students' learning and well-being *and to enhance the teacher's cultural awareness.*

Explanation: We chose to stress the importance of teachers experiencing the cultural life of their communities so that they might appreciate cultural diversity and utilize culture as a source of teaching and learning.

Philosophical Interpretation of Standards

As our department continuously worked on clarifying our constructivist philosophy and standards, it became a logical next step to connect the two. We asked ourselves questions like these: Upon what instructional strategies would a constructivist rely the most (Standard #4)? How would a constructivist best communicate in a classroom (Standard #6)? Thus, in 1994, we wrote our philosophy statement as a constructivist interpretation of our ten standards (Campbell et al., 1994). In our current philosophy document each standard is presented in turn, with our explanation of how each standard might be demonstrated by a constructivist teacher. (A sample standard explanation is provided in Figure 1.2.)

FIGURE 1.2   Sample Chapter in Our Philosophy Document

The Constructivist Teacher

<u>Knowledge of Subject Matter</u>

Standard #1: The teacher understands the central concepts, tools of inquiry, and structures of the disciplines taught at the Early Childhood/Elementary levels.

Constructivists believe that learners construct knowledge by interacting with their environment. The role of the teacher in this model is to help learners build their own knowledge by acting on materials and engaging in meaningful experiences.

One might mistakenly believe that knowledge of subject matter is less important in the constructivist model of learning than in more traditional approaches to teaching. It is our contention, however, that to instruct successfully in a constructivist classroom, teachers must possess an in-depth understanding of major concepts, assumptions, debates, processes of inquiry, and ways of knowing that are central to the disciplines they teach.

When learning is viewed as the construction of knowledge, rather than the transference of knowledge, holistic activities in which complex forms of knowledge are presented and action is required of the child seem most appropriate (Schickendanz et al., 1990). First-hand experiences are preferred over "teacher telling," practicing of discrete skills, or learning isolated pieces of knowledge. Integration of content areas within the elementary classroom is needed to ensure that the experiences learners receive are meaningful and purposeful. Thus, in the constructivist classroom the teacher must possess sufficient subject matter knowledge to create interdisciplinary learning experiences that allow students to integrate knowledge, skills, and methods of inquiry from several subject areas.

Knowledge of subject matter also implies an understanding of the methods of inquiry used in the various disciplines. Suchman (1964) developed a strategy commonly referred to as inquiry training. In inquiry training, students experience the same process that scientists go through when attempting to explain a puzzling phenomenon. Employing methods such as inquiry training in the constructivist classroom allows teachers to engage learners in generating knowledge and testing hypotheses according to the methods of inquiry and standards of evidence used in the science discipline.

Having learners act on materials and engage in meaningful experiences is a central concept in the constructivist theory, so it is critical that the teacher evaluate resources and curriculum materials for their comprehensiveness,

Continued

FIGURE 1.2 *Continued*

accuracy, and usefulness for representing particular ideas and concepts. Subject matter knowledge is essential for the selection and evaluation of curriculum materials and resources. Knowledge of subject matter is universally considered an essential attribute for effective teaching. It is no less important for the constructivist teacher to possess in-depth knowledge of subject matter than it would be for a teacher employing a traditional approach.

Maintaining Focus through Portfolios

We have found that the most effective way to maintain the focus of our students and faculty on our standards or goals is to use professional portfolios. Our students document their professional growth in portfolios organized around our adaptations of INTASC standards. Portfolios are divided into ten sections, one for each of our standards. Throughout their professional training, students collect, generate, and organize documents that give evidence of learning and competence in these ten standards. This makes possible the authentic assessment of student performance. Furthermore, students begin to discern how various courses, assignments, and experiences fit together. Professional portfolios for preservice teachers make the vision of the program visible to faculty and students alike. In addition to maintaining everyone's focus on the program standards, this type of student portfolio accomplishes three other important outcomes related to evaluation, student control of learning, and employment.

First, portfolios facilitate program evaluation. Your faculty can determine whether you have met your goals as a teacher education program because patterns evolve as students create their portfolios. Students are able to document some of the standards more easily and more meaningfully than others. Serious gaps become apparent. These data inform faculty as to how to change courses, assignments, and syllabi. They also help balance the assignments within your program of studies. (Appendix A shows the artifacts checklist that we use to collect relevant data.)

Second, portfolios enable students to be more active, reflective, and autonomous in their learning, both during their preparation program and throughout their careers. Every portfolio is a balance of documents. Some documents are assigned by faculty as portfolio entries, others are class assignments chosen by students, and still others are created by students to describe significant out-of-class activities. As students select items to be included and create documents to showcase strengths or improve weaknesses, they gain considerable control over their own learning. This is especially true when you as a faculty choose to take an enabling approach to portfolio work. As enablers, your role becomes that of helping students show what they know and can do. An enabling model rejects the approach of using portfolios to "catch" students on what they do not know. In an enabling model, students are more likely to become lifelong learners who know strategies for taking control of their ongoing growth throughout their professional lives.

Third, portfolios provide students with professional marketing and credentialing tools after graduation. They give prospective employers compelling evidence of teaching skills, achievements, and experiences. They go far beyond a traditional résumé in revealing the unique qualities of the applicant. Likewise, many credentialing bodies require evidence of performance competence that could be best presented in a portfolio.

COMMUNICATING THE VISION

Once your teacher education program reaches consensus on a vision, you face the challenge of effectively communicating that vision. In order to successfully implement a portfolio development system, it may be helpful to designate one course or develop a seminar as a keystone for introducing the program philosophy and standards and the portfolio concept. When an introduction to portfolio work is embedded in a course, three important goals are added to the course content goals:

1. Students will understand the philosophical underpinnings of the theory that the teacher education program has adopted, how it compares to other theories, and why a philosophy of teaching is important.

2. Students study the meaning of the standards for teachers that are adopted by the program, why standards are important, and how the chosen standards connect to the program philosophy.
3. Students begin to consider the multiple purposes of portfolios. They learn the step-by-step process of preparing portfolios. They practice some of the needed skills such as writing clear descriptions of experiences and thoughtful analyses of the value of various professional activities. They are taught how this work relates to ongoing professional reflection. The opportunity for beginning students enrolled in this course to interact with advanced students around portfolio development is a valuable part of this component.

Meeting these goals can generally be accomplished within 12 to 15 hours of instruction time; therefore, if you wish, this orientation could be handled in a seminar. However, we have had success with providing this orientation in a course we call "Instructional Strategies," which is required of all students as they enter our teacher education program. As students spend the remaining hours of instructional time in the course investigating research and accumulated knowledge on competent teaching, they continuously make connections to philosophies of teaching and to standards. In this sense the teaching of philosophical orientations, standards for excellent teaching, and the importance of ongoing reflectiveness and documentation are embedded throughout the entirety of such a course. By way of illustration, we will describe how each of the three goals has been achieved in our Elementary/Early Childhood teacher education program.

Students Learn the Philosophical Orientation

Students enrolled in an entry-level course in our department are generally sophomores. At their stage of development it is often difficult for them to understand the need for a chosen philosophical orientation. Therefore, we have found the most helpful approach to teaching our constructivist philosophy is to compare it to other theories, such as behaviorism, nativism, and humanism. Students begin to see how one's philosophical assumptions influence decisions about how to organize the curriculum, manage the classroom, and choose a repertoire of instructional strategies.

This comparative approach is especially important in our case because we have many students who are dual majors in Elementary/Special Education or Early Childhood/Special Education. At our university the Special Education Department advocates a behaviorist orientation. At times, students with dual majors feel confused as they move from department to department; therefore, we must give them a sound orientation to the assumptions and frame of reference of each theory.

Sometimes students in this course, especially those with dual majors, are in conflict about their own beliefs. They need to be encouraged to embrace their questions and welcome them as unique opportunities for learning. They seem to need help in accepting feelings of conflict, confusion, and irresolution. Clearly this entry-level course is a time when they begin to understand critical differences between broad theories; constructing for themselves their own philosophies of teaching will require many more experiences with children, classrooms, and educational ideas.

We attempt to reassure our students that our goal is not to create constructivist clones. We are quite comfortable with students eventually constructing a theory different from ours. We do, believe, however, that the work of reflection and philosophy building is essential for every teacher. Further, it is our goal that every teacher who graduates from our program has a good understanding of the critical principles of constructivist teaching and has a wide repertoire of appropriate constructivist strategies. The faculty-authored *A Constructivist Model for Teaching* (Campbell et al., 1994) is the primary textbook for this part of the course. As shown in Figure 1.2, it provides a constructivist interpretation of our ten standards.

Students Explore Standards for Teaching

Majors in our department need to become very familiar with our chosen standards because everything we do in the department is based upon them. To a large extent our standards determine the content of our courses; they are the focus for student portfolios, and they are the basis for the evaluation of students in field courses and student teaching.

During our entry-level course, instruction on the standards focuses on these questions:

1. Why are standards necessary?
2. What are our chosen standards trying to communicate? What do they mean?
3. What is a constructivist interpretation of each standard?
4. How do these standards guide the work of the department and each individual student?
5. What would achievement of each standard look like in actual behavior; i.e., what are some behavioral indicators?
6. How can growth in achieving standards be measured and documented?

Students Learn about Portfolio Development

We recommend two resources to communicate to students the nature of portfolios and the portfolio assessment system. The first is a set of guidelines in portfolio development prepared to use with your students. This set of guidelines should present your rationale for portfolio development as well as step-by-step practical procedures on how you would like students to organize their professional portfolios. Chapter 2 summarizes some of the information that is most beneficial for students to have in program guidelines for portfolio development. More details on creating portfolios, as well as an explanation of the INTASC standards, are included in the published manual that we use in our program (Campbell et al., 1997).

A second resource is sample portfolios. Model portfolios might be maintained by the program. Other sample portfolios can be shared by advanced students with beginning students. In our program, student teachers make a presentation of their portfolios one day each semester. They begin their presentations by reflecting upon their experiences as former students in this class, and they suggest how students can use their preservice experiences on campus and in the schools and community to enhance their training and portfolios.

They offer examples of early portfolio entries and reinforce the concept of revisiting and revising the portfolio. This session is beneficial for students in the Instructional Strategies classes, who can visualize how current work is contributing to the attainment of professional standards.

On the day that seniors visit the Instructional Strategies classes, they serve as consultants when not making formal presentations to a class. Several classrooms are designated as consultation rooms. Student teachers display their portfolios and work with individuals and small groups of preservice students, advising them in how to enhance and use their portfolios. This arrangement produces a nonthreatening environment in which preservice students can interact with peers, asking questions and sharing ideas that they may not be comfortable articulating with a faculty member or administrator.

In our entry-level course, instruction on portfolio development also focuses on defining attributes of a portfolio, clarifying the values and purposes that a portfolio can serve, and explaining how a portfolio is organized.

Attributes of a Portfolio
Students come to realize that a portfolio is not a scrapbook of college course assignments and memorabilia. Rather, we characterize a presentation portfolio as an organized documentation of growth and achievement that provides tangible evidence of the attainment of professional knowledge, skills, and dispositions. Each portfolio is goal-driven, original, and reflective.

We clarify for students the difference between a working portfolio and a presentation portfolio. Working portfolios include the complete collection of work samples in unabridged form. This type of portfolio may require file drawers or boxes, as it might include complete units, art project collections, and teacher-made materials, for example. A working portfolio also includes uncompleted projects. In contrast, a presentation portfolio is a carefully selected, streamlined, and organized collection of work samples and other pieces of evidence prepared to share with others, especially with those who make judgments about one's achieved competence.

Values and Purposes of a Portfolio

Barton and Collins suggest that "the first and most significant act of portfolio preparation is the decision of the purposes of the portfolio" (1993, p.103). When reflecting on the value and benefits of portfolios, students quickly recognize the potential of a portfolio as an employment or credentialing tool. However, we contend that students who view portfolios only as products will become teachers who use them in a limited way. Thus, we have sought to instill in our students an understanding of portfolios as part of a process of monitoring ongoing professional growth. Only after some experience do students realize how portfolios give greater self-understanding and are therefore effective tools for goal setting and self-directed learning. Students eventually use their portfolios to plan their professional development with other professionals, such as cooperating teachers and professors. It is our goal that they will continue to view portfolios as part of a learning process when they become teachers.

Figure 1.3 shows some sample responses from a recent survey of juniors in our program. The survey question asked, "How have you benefited from the process of portfolio development?" These responses indicate that students became aware of the full range of benefits of portfolio work.

Portfolio Organization

In the entry-level class, students are taught the elements of an organized professional portfolio. In our program it is essential that portfolio work be geared toward standards for excellence. It is not enough to present letters of recommendation, evaluations, lesson and unit plans, and documentation of out-of-class professional activities. Such artifacts need to be connected to professional standards in a meaningful way. To facilitate this connection, students are required to have a labeled section for each standard. Further, for each artifact chosen for a presentation portfolio, students create a cover sheet with a rationale that explains clearly what the document is, answers why the artifact was chosen to document that particular standard, and provides a reflection on how the experience represented by the artifact facilitated progress in teaching skills.

FIGURE 1.3   Responses from a Survey of Juniors in Our Program

Question: How have you benefited from the process of portfolio development?

"It has helped me to build confidence in myself as an educator."

"Portfolio development has helped me to identify my strengths and weaknesses in the areas covered by the ten standards."

"I have become more aware of what future employers may be looking for in an employee."

"It is nice to be able to look back at everything I have accomplished throughout my college career."

"The portfolio has helped me become more organized. It has helped me set goals and achieve them. I have a basis for my future in education."

"By having specific outcomes to accomplish I am able to see exactly what areas of preparation I need to work on to become a constructivist teacher."

"I feel that the development of the portfolio has helped me see the importance of my work."

"It made me strive to do my best work possible."

"It helped me see the value of the assignments that I have completed in my classes. I take away more meaning from my work."

"It has shown me how what I have learned all fits together."

"It is a self portrait . . ."

"I have gained tremendous knowledge concerning the standards for educators."

"The portfolio development itself is a means of becoming professional. The ten standards enable me to reflect upon my work continuously as I develop into a teacher. The standards have helped me focus my learning . . . ."

"I feel a sense of accomplishment . . . . Being able to see your own growth and achievement is very exciting. Developing this portfolio has made me quite aware of the hard work that goes into teaching."

The rationale cover sheets not only help future readers understand the portfolio document, but they also help the students learn to be more reflective about their work.

While it is critical that students understand all the features that portfolios will have in common in the program, it is equally important that they are aware of the rich possibilities for making their own portfolios unique and creative. We have found several good ways to do this. One is to encourage students to use a wide variety of document types. Our faculty brainstormed a list of fifty possible artifacts, which are defined for students in our guidelines publication and are reproduced in Appendix B. A second way we highlight various possibilities for portfolio documents is to have students select assignments to include. Also, they generate documents to reflect valuable out-of-class experiences. Students who have been active in professional organizations, who have coaching or camp counseling experiences, or who have had prior careers are shown how to reflect upon and showcase the learning that these activities have fostered. Thus, every portfolio is unique because every student's experiences are unique. Another way we help students individualize their portfolios is to encourage them to use selected photos, personal art, clip art, and graphics to give their portfolios visual impact. Reviewers find such portfolios inviting.

CONCLUSION

It is our position that a high-quality teacher education program is one in which faculty members have asked themselves, "What kind of teacher do we want a graduate of our program to be?" This goal-oriented focus helps everyone involved to be clear about the process of educating future teachers. Gaining this vision and then communicating it is the starting point for developing a program that emphasizes teacher performance.

The next chapter will show you the role that portfolios play in such a program. The importance of establishing guidelines for creating portfolios is emphasized.

▶ 2

Guidelines for Portfolio Development

Students who are expected to create professional portfolios need to know the parameters of that requirement. Written guidelines need to be established, shared, evaluated for effectiveness, and revised. This chapter will summarize some of the content generally offered in such a set of guidelines. A much more detailed description of our recommended guidelines for prospective teachers is found in *How to Develop a Professional Portfolio: A Manual for Teachers* (Campbell et al., 1997). You may find that the recommendations given there serve the needs of your teacher education students, especially if you plan to use INTASC standards.

RATIONALE FOR PORTFOLIO DEVELOPMENT

The first thing your students need to know is the rationale of your program for portfolio development. Goals for portfolio work vary from one institution to another, and your goals need to be set forth for students. You will also need to address your particular definition of a professional teacher portfolio. Your rationale might attempt to give your students a picture of various ways their portfolios could be used and various audiences for their portfolios. This would also be an appropriate section in which to give students tips on how to effectively present their portfolios to various audiences such as interviewers, mentors, supervisors, and credentialing agents.

EXPLANATION OF STANDARDS

Not only do your students need to become familiar with chosen standards; they also need to gain an in-depth understanding of them. Entire courses and a multitude of books have been devoted to the issues inherent in most professional standards for teachers. Thus, in-depth understanding is a career-long goal. However, some beginning attempt at explaining the standards needs to be offered in your portfolio guidelines. We have found four strategies for instructing students in the meaning of standards. The first is to provide expanded explanations of each standard in a few paragraphs. A second helpful strategy is to provide scenarios giving examples of situations in which professional activities lead to achievement in some aspect of a standard. A third strategy is to break down the standards, which are broad and multifaceted, into major elements. The last strategy is to provide a sample list of behavioral indicators of the standard. Such a list is generated by asking, "What would competence in this standard look like in actual teacher behavior?" Figure 2.1 is an explanation of an INTASC standard using these four strategies.

LIST OF ARTIFACT POSSIBILITIES

Another content item in the written portfolio guidelines is a list of possible artifacts for portfolios. Such suggestions are provided so students will grasp the range of possibilities and move away from overreliance on a few kinds of documents. You could simply provide students with this list; however, we found that it was more helpful to annotate the list with a definition of each document type and an explanation of the teaching skills and knowledge that this artifact may reflect. Appendix B is a listing of fifty artifact possibilities that we have distributed to our students (Campbell et al., 1997).

FIGURE 2.1   Four Ways of Explaining Standards to Students in a Teacher Education Program

Standard #5

The teacher uses an understanding of individual and group motivation and behavior to create a learning environment that encourages positive social interaction, active engagement in learning, and self-motivation.

Explanation of Standard #5

Effective teachers work in many ways to build positive classroom interactions. These teachers recognize that involving students in this endeavor not only promotes growth in personal and social responsibility, but also enhances the development of democratic and social values. Group rapport is enhanced as students and teachers work cooperatively to establish classroom norms and rules. Teaching and modeling effective problem-solving techniques such as conflict resolution provide motivation for learning, positive social interaction among children, and positive self-esteem for all. Thus, effective teachers strive to create a learning community that fosters group decision making, collaboration as well as individual responsibility, and self-directed learning.

Teachers interested in building and sustaining a positive learning climate are aware of the range of behavioral phenomena confronting them. They recognize that there are situations in which some students are unable to function within the parameters established by the group. In these instances, teachers must rely upon their knowledge of the principles and strategies of behavior management and issues related to all aspects of behavior management. As reflective practitioners, teachers use this knowledge of theory, along with their classroom experiences, to construct an ever evolving philosophy of student motivation and management. This philosophy is specific enough to guide classroom actions, yet flexible enough to accommodate the individual needs of students. Therefore, effective classroom managers understand the need to be able to define problems, identify alternatives, choose a course of action and a plan for implementation, and consider the possible consequences of a given action. The teaching scenario that follows shows how a preservice teacher was able to assess his ability to create a positive learning environment, and to modify his teaching behaviors to improve the climate of his classroom.

Teaching Scenario That Depicts Standard #5

While enrolled in an early field experience class, Michael has the opportunity to spend a few hours every week in a day care classroom working with children ages 3 to 5. Michael soon realizes that these young children can be very impetuous and need a great deal of support from teachers in developing self-control and learning how to function in a group.

The college instructor in the class addresses "Promoting Positive Guidance" as one of her seminar topics. In class, Michael and his classmates practice phrasing requests and directions to young children in a positive, encouraging way that invites children's cooperation and teaches them problem-solving and negotiating skills.

Continued

FIGURE 2.1   *Continued*

Michael values this instruction because he realizes that he has a tendency to be directive and often negative with children, using a great many "don'ts." Michael decides to systematically practice these positive guidance techniques in the classroom with children.

He asks a fellow classmate who is doing fieldwork with him at the day care center to observe and record any negative, discouraging, or demanding comments that he makes to the children. After receiving her observations, Michael reflects on how he could have communicated those same requests to the children in a positive, encouraging way. Gradually, over time, Michael finds he is gaining in his ability to spontaneously use positive verbal guidance. He is also becoming more likely to invite problem solving rather than solve problems through correcting children.

Michael is proud of this growth and can see how his behavior is resulting in better rapport with these children and is helping to create a more positive social climate. Michael decides to document this work. He includes in his portfolio a videotape of his interactions with the group as well as anecdotal records of his growth based on the observations of his classmate.

Elements of the Standard

Establishing and teaching standards for behavior
Teaching and modeling problem solving
Teaching democratic group decision making and collaboration
Responding to student behavior
Treating children fairly and respectfully
Preventing management problems
Managing learning time effectively
Organizing the physical environment to actively engage students
Using positive verbal guidance

Sample Behavioral Indicators of One of the Elements of Standard #5

Element: Using positive verbal guidance

Behavioral Indicators:

The student teacher verbally recognizes children's positive efforts and contributions.

The student teacher discusses positive expectations with children.

The student teacher verbalizes the value and relevance of learning activities.

The student teacher converses with individual students regularly.

The student teacher uses humor to diffuse difficult situations, when appropriate.

The student teacher addresses individual progress rather than comparing students.

The student teacher encourages cooperation rather than competition.

FIGURE 2.1 *Continued*

The student teacher makes use of open-ended questions to solicit students' ideas and opinions.

The student teacher tells children what to do rather than what not to do when their behavior is inappropriate.

The student teacher helps children generate solutions to problems and conflicts.

The student teacher models for students appropriate ways to express anger and frustration.

DESCRIPTION OF THE ORGANIZATION SYSTEM

A portfolio is not merely a collection of course projects, assignments, videotapes, and pictures designed to impress someone. If it is to meet its full potential, a portfolio must be organized, goal-driven, performance-based evidence that indicates the attainment of the knowledge, skills, and attitudes needed to be a teacher. Some teacher educators believe that students should impose their own organizational schemes on their portfolio documentation. Certainly when a portfolio is being designed solely as a marketing tool, this might be desirable. It would allow for the greatest flexibility and enhance opportunities for individuality and creativity.

However, when portfolios are being used by a teacher education program to focus the efforts of both faculty and students on achieving standards for professional performance, it makes more sense to organize at least most of the portfolio around the chosen standards. An easy way for your students to do this is to divide the portfolio into labeled sections, one for each of the standards. Many teacher educators set forth additional requirements such as beginning the portfolio with an autobiography or letter of introduction. Some require a personal philosophy of education, a demographic description of the communities and schools in which the student has had experience, a culminating project, or a piece of classroom research. If you wish to specify such requirements, your students need to know them from the outset. We recommend that, after students have winnowed presentation portfolios from working portfolios, they include a final reflection, rationale, and table of contents. This encourages reflection on the important growth that has occurred, makes clear the areas of need for further professional development, and enables students to more effectively share their work with others.

COVER SHEETS AND RATIONALE

Artifacts or documents that stand alone in a portfolio without explanation of context and reflection of value can be confusing or even misleading. In addition, not requiring such reflection robs the students of a most valuable learning tool. Your students should preface each document selected for inclusion in a presentation portfolio with some identifying information and a rationale that justifies the value of the document and the experience it represents. We recommend that rationales answer at least three important questions:

1. What is the artifact?
2. How does it relate to this particular standard?
3. What does it say about one's growing competence?

We also like the three questions suggested by Van Wagenen and Hibbard (1998):

1. "What?"
2. "So what?"
3. "Now what?"

To use these questions, the student would first summarize the artifact that documents the experience, in order to answer the question "What?" Second, the student would reflect on what he or she learned and how this leads to meeting the standard, which answers the question "So what?" And third, the student would address implications for further learning needed and set forth refinements or adaptations, in order to answer "Now what?"

If you believe that your students could benefit from more introspection, you may also wish to require an expanded reflection page

---

FIGURE 2.2   **Sample of a Cover Sheet that Contains a Rationale**

Artifact for Standard #5: Classroom Management Skills

Name of Artifact: Evidence of Positive Verbal Guidance

Date: March 4, 2000

Course: ECE 203, Field Experiences with Young Children

Rationale:

   I have chosen to use two artifacts that indicate the growth I have attained in understanding how to create a positive learning environment with very young children. The first is anecdotal records of interactions I had in a classroom of 3- to 5-year-olds and my reflections on the outcomes of those interactions. The anecdotal records show growth in my ability to formulate positive, encouraging requests and responses to children. The second is a videotape of myself near the end of the field experience showing informal conversations with children and a teacher-directed activity. In this videotape I demonstrate my ability to gain children's cooperation by the way I speak with them. I also demonstrate how I help the children solve problems with their peers, encouraging cooperation rather than taking over the situation. The strategies I am employing lead to positive social interaction and positive individual and group motivation.

---

for each major artifact, especially for performance assessments. Standardized formats for cover sheets with rationales and reflection pages are very helpful to students and to those who review their portfolios. Figure 2.2 gives a sample of a cover sheet.

CONCLUSION

In this chapter we discussed five necessary components of program guidelines on portfolio building. They are (1) a rationale for portfolio development, (2) explanations of the chosen standards, (3) a list of artifact possibilities, (4) a description of an overall organizational system for the portfolio, and (5) the requirement of cover sheets with rationales. Chapter 3 will explain the role of performance assessments in the development of portfolios in a teacher education program.

Ensuring Quality in Student Learning through Performance Assessments and Rubrics

Portfolios, by themselves, do not guarantee that students learn what is important. Indeed, according to Newmann and Wehlage (1993), unless students' portfolios are guided by "substantive, worthwhile ends," a portfolio system alone, without the support of purposeful documents, could actually "undermine meaningful learning" (p. 8). It is important to remember that the "objective is not to create outstanding portfolios, but rather to cultivate outstanding teaching and learning" (Wolf, 1996, p. 37). Thus, a portfolio system necessitates a reexamination of the way in which students' learning is assessed. A mere collection of test scores, letters of recommendation, and traditional assignments would not fulfill the intended function of the portfolio, which is to serve as a dynamic, flexible documentation of student growth.

This was made obvious to us in the first year of this endeavor. On a pilot basis we began to ask students to organize their portfolios, inserting documents that they had saved from their course work in our program. After examining these portfolios, one professor remarked, politely but candidly, "But there's nothing here. These portfolios have nice organization with no substance!"

This forced us to think about what we were asking our students to do. After much discussion, reexamination, and exploration we decided that performance-based assessments provide the authentic learning and purposeful documents that we needed.

We have found that students' portfolios that are built upon performance-based assessments can provide three things. First, they allow teacher education students to demonstrate—for themselves as well as for others—how well they are meeting individual course objectives as well as program standards in ways that indicate their ability to apply what they know. Second, they allow faculty members to determine how well their students are learning what they believe is important for them to know. And third, they allow teacher educators to assess their programs, in that faculty members can collectively determine how well they are actually meeting their own goals as a department. Thus, performance-based assessments can help to ensure high-quality learning in a teacher education program.

Based on this premise, performance assessments are extremely important parts of your students' portfolios. But they are not the only type of document that could be included in a portfolio. Students can create their own documents, or they can use more traditional types of assignments from other courses as artifacts. It is important to establish criteria for the quality and quantity of the types of documents included, especially if portfolios are being used as assessments in the evaluation of student performance throughout the program. If there are no expectations for the overall product, then it is quite possible for students to create mediocre portfolios. Some might be skimpy, containing very few documents. Others might contain documents that are course-embedded, yet are poorly done. Still others might be little more than large scrapbooks of neatly organized course work. Without a consistent set of criteria, many questions remain unanswered: How many documents should students' portfolios contain? Should all documents be free of mechanical errors? With how many artifacts should each departmental standard be documented? Thus, rubrics are also very important for ensuring quality of learning in your teacher education program, because they outline criteria for excellence, ensuring that both students and faculty are aware of what is expected in portfolio work.

The account that follows defines the types of performance assessments that we suggest, describes how they can be used in your teacher education program, and explains how you can maintain quality of learning through their use. Then, rubrics for portfolio development are defined and discussed in terms of how they can facilitate a program-wide effort to ensure quality.

FUNCTIONS OF PERFORMANCE ASSESSMENTS

There are many reasons for assigning tasks in a teacher preparation course. Homework assignments, readings, outside projects, class assignments, and written reports reflect course objectives and discrete skills that are necessary for teaching. Traditional types of assignments such as these serve a useful purpose in that they assess or give practice in a focused manner. However, college students sometimes see these assignments as "busywork" because they are narrow and often do not connect to real-life experiences in practice. We have found that when such assignments are the only ones required of students, they do not receive the opportunity to view course work as an integral part of their professional growth.

Performance assessment projects or tasks differ from these traditional assignments in that they are broader in scope, are more authentic, are "more likely to elicit a student's full repertoire of skills" (Gardner, 1991, p. 93), and reflect a range of goals that you want your students to meet. According to the Association for Supervision and Curriculum Development (ASCD), when students are asked to complete performance assessments, they see that the assignments contain multiple, coherent components that have clear purposes. Such projects or tasks make connections to the students' interests and are culminating in that they synthesize learning in all or part of the course (ASCD, 1997).

As vital measurements of the professional growth of preservice teachers, performance assessments do the following: (1) reflect the standards or outcomes of the teacher education program, (2) synthesize all or part of the learning in a course, (3) reflect the real-life work of teaching, (4) require revision of written work, (5) allow choices or reflect student interest, and (6) facilitate professional self-reflection. Each of these functions will be discussed separately, and for each, a set of questions that can guide you in creating performance assessments for courses in your teacher education program will be given.

Reflecting Program Standards or Outcomes

A project designed for any course in the program should reflect at least one—and many times several—of the standards that have been adopted by your teacher education program. This helps to ensure that your students are indeed learning what you believe is important for preservice teachers to know and that their documentation of learning reflects the classroom context (Meisels, 1996–1997). In addition, students' portfolios inevitably document the work of your faculty as well as the work of the students. Program evaluation will become a more meaningful process as the faculty members in your department look at the growing documentation of your students' attainment of standards or outcomes.

When designing performance assessments for each of your courses, you can use these questions to determine whether they reflect your program standards or outcomes:

1. Which standards or outcomes are most important for this course?
2. What types of tasks would ensure that your students are able to meet these standards or outcomes?
3. What kinds of learning does this course require? How does the project or task reflect that?
4. What kinds of learning does the professor who teaches this course value? How does the project or task reflect that?
5. What models of teaching will facilitate the desired learning?

Synthesizing Course Learning

Performance assessment projects or tasks are designed to synthesize all or part of the learning that takes place in a course. "Genuine mastery of a given body of content" (Nordquist, 1993, p. 64) is reflected in these assessments. The task or project is an assessment of performance only if it can be done well by students who have truly learned course content (ASCD, 1997). This makes them different from typical skill-oriented assignments in that they allow students to show a broad range of abilities associated with the content of the course. They drive the curriculum; a performance assessment always takes over at least a portion of the course. To determine what is to be included in a performance assessment task or assignment, you need to determine the most essential concepts of the course, then devise a task that shows that your students know these concepts. Some projects can be completed and evaluated in a series of steps, which allows students to utilize several capabilities and receive feedback along the way. The formative nature of these projects or tasks helps you and your students focus on the process of learning as well as its product.

Questions to ask while developing projects or tasks that synthesize learning include:

1. What are the most important things that your students should know and be able to do as a result of this course?
2. How can your students apply relevant course content to create something new?
3. What student behavior would assure you that your students really understand this concept?
4. Is the task or project worthy of the time and energy required to complete it?
5. Does the task have sufficient depth and breadth to "allow valid generalizations about overall student competence?" (Wiggins, 1992, p. 26)
6. What knowledge or skills from this course can be used as "a tool for fashioning a performance or product?" (Wiggins, 1992, p. 27)

Reflecting the Real-Life Work of Teaching

Performance-based assessments are designed to measure whether students can apply their understanding in authentic contexts (McTighe, 1996–1997). Using performance-based assessments means that the curriculum must focus on real-world problem solving and that it is no longer simply content to be covered, but consists of desired "performances of understanding" (p. 8). Your students will be practicing the abilities that will be demanded of them as teachers. Thus, you may find that the make-up of some teacher preparation courses will change, reflecting the true nature of schooling. For example, we found that our partnerships with local schools and day care centers, while they had been in place for quite some time, became stronger, giving our students authentic contexts within which to work, observe, and study. As a result, one of these schools became a Professional Development School (PDS). Our PDS is a place where students who are in our field, methods, and student teaching classes can participate in authentic classroom experiences with professionals who share our philosophy and our commitment to portfolio development.

To help determine authenticity, ask these questions about the tasks or projects that you design:

1. How can your students show their achieved competence in a way similar to how people use knowledge and skills in the real world?
2. What kinds of tasks, "performed all the time by [inservice] professionals . . . , can be adapted for use?" (Wiggins, 1992, p. 29)
3. How can this task or project actually be used in a real-life situation?

Requiring Revision of Written Work

Performance-based assessments in a teacher education program need to reflect the work of a professional. Such work is not written once, then graded and forgotten. You will not only assign these tasks and projects, but you will also assume responsibility for helping students develop the required skills and dispositions that they need to show their understanding of the concepts you are teaching. When students are asked to revise their work until it is acceptable, there is a shared responsibility for making sure that understanding has evolved and can be articulated. As students draft, edit, revise, and revise again, you will be facilitating this process by making suggestions, giving feedback, and making sure that learning is happening. Such a process does not merely focus on the mechanics of the students' papers; instead, it holds you responsible as a teacher to ensure students' learning. This can be a frustrating enterprise for both students and faculty who are not accustomed to nurturing ongoing work. It can also be difficult in the sense that many college courses last only a few weeks, and much content needs to be addressed in that short amount of time.

All of this means that it is important to choose and plan performance assessment tasks or projects carefully. The project or task needs to reflect the content of the course; in addition, ample time must be allowed for the revision process. Thus, when you assign large projects that address lots of content, you must carefully plan your course outline and schedule time for students to learn the content, apply it to their project, receive feedback from you, and revise the project—sometimes more than once.

Peer editing is a vital part of the revision process. Asking peers whom they trust to edit, give feedback, and make suggestions gives students valuable collaborative experiences; in addition, it accomplishes the practical purpose of helping students purge minor errors from their work before submitting it to their professor.

A performance assessment product that has evolved over time, with opportunities for revision and feedback, gives students a clear sense of cumulative learning. It also challenges you, the professor, to be truly facilitative in your approach to teaching. As you design performance assessments, you can use these questions about focusing on the process of completing a task or project:

1. Have there been stages to these projects and opportunities for your students to receive feedback?
2. How can time constraints be accommodated when focusing on the revision process?

3. How can you ensure "expert judgments" of your students' work? (Diez & Moon, 1992, p. 38)
4. How can you—and others who review your students' work— provide high-quality feedback?
5. What will count as acceptable performance? (Diez & Moon, 1992)

Providing for Student Choice and Interest

One of the features of performance assessments that stands apart from traditional assignments is the element of choice or connection to students' interests. Because one of the reasons for creating portfolios is to allow students to have some autonomy over their learning, providing for choice or interest is important. You can allow students to choose some aspects of their projects, such as the topic they wish to research, the children's literature they will use, the number of children they need to work with, the collaborative learning group they will join, or perhaps even the type of project they will complete. Doing this is powerfully motivating because the students feel that they have some control over what they are learning, yet the content and structure of the course is not out of the hands of the professor. It is also a more meaningful way for students to learn because they can structure their projects to meet their own needs.

We have tried many different ways of providing for choice and interest and have found that the nature of the course and the maturity level of the students are important. Sometimes performance assessments need to remain quite structured so that objectives and standards can be met. With these assignments you may want to have the students make smaller decisions such as which children's book to use in a lesson or which collaborative group to join. Other performance assessments may depend completely upon the students' choices. For example, graduate students may participate in problem-solving conferences with the professor and create their own projects that will help them meet some personal and professional goals.

Questions to guide you as you think about allowing for choice and interest are:

1. What is the purpose of this project or task? How will student choices reflect this purpose?
2. What parts of the project or task must be chosen by the professor in order to meet objectives and standards?
3. How can you help students make wise decisions in their completion of projects or tasks?
4. What parts of the project could be supported with limited choices, such as allowing students to choose from a selection of topics, resources, or titles?

Facilitating Professional Self-Reflection

One mark of the professional is the ability to reflect upon one's actions and learning, then make decisions based on that reflection. Performance assessments should help your students to do just that. We suggest two ways to accomplish this.

First, require self-reflection as a part of the project or task. It should be shown in the body of the assignment. There must be some reflection on what was learned, how this assignment helped the student to grow professionally, and any decisions that could be made about what to do in a similar situation in the future.

Second, require students to write a rationale for each of the documents they include in their portfolio. This statement explains why the document is important in their portfolio and how it reflects an understanding of the standard or outcome under which it is "filed," or with which it corresponds. Many documents demonstrate attainments in multiple standards. Our students are asked to choose a primary standard for filing a document that reflects what they gained most from the experience. In the rationale, students reflect on the connections they see between their work and the selected standard. If you wish, a rationale might also address how multiple standards are met. Self-reflection increases students' involvement in their own learning because they begin to perceive the purpose for their assignments. When their assignments have more meaning to them, they are more willing to complete them to the best of their abilities.

When designing tasks or projects to contain a self-reflection component, you may find these questions useful:

1. How can you help students articulate the meaning and significance of their tasks or projects in relation to the course content?
2. How can you help students explain how their projects or tasks relate to program standards or outcomes?
3. How can you help students explain how their projects or tasks have helped them grow professionally?

TYPES OF PERFORMANCE ASSESSMENTS

The nature of performance assessments varies, depending on the type of course being taught as well as the professor's teaching style. Two types of performance assessments can be included in the program: performance assessment projects and performance assessment tasks. Both of these are explained here.

Performance Assessment Projects

Some projects are inclusive, reflecting nearly all of the objectives and desired outcomes of the course. This type of project usually takes a semester to complete, and in fact, a single project often controls the entire course. Its purpose is to synthesize all the learning that has taken place in the course. Often several program standards can be met with this type of project.

An example of one such project that we use is the creation of the "theme box," which is a complete resource unit of materials, activity ideas, and trade books that reflect a chosen theme. It synthesizes the learning that has taken place in a course called "Thematic Teaching." Other examples of projects include case studies, research papers, and unit plans.

Such projects usually work well in courses that we call "focus-oriented" and that are designed to address a specific issue in depth and at length. They would also work well for you if you are interested in having students create a single product that reflects the merging of several course objectives.

Performance Assessment Tasks

Assignments that reflect a limited number of course objectives, standards, or outcomes are called performance assessment tasks. Each of these tasks is less time-consuming than a project, yet is valuable because it authentically assesses learning on some important aspect of the course. You may require several tasks throughout the semester, so that many objectives are met.

An example of a performance task, assigned in our required introductory course called "Instructional Strategies," is a time-on-task study. This task requires the students to visit a classroom and record the total amount of time on learning tasks that a single child exhibits. This rather specific, yet powerful, exercise also involves the student's interpretation of the results. Other examples of tasks include lesson plan components, memos or letters, position papers, and journal article critiques. Courses that lend themselves to the assignment of performance assessment tasks are what we call "survey-oriented" and are designed to address a wide range of teaching skills and capabilities. Such tasks would work well for you if you are interested in assessing only a few objectives, standards, or outcomes at a time and want to focus on these goals in a detailed way.

HOW PERFORMANCE ASSESSMENTS MAINTAIN QUALITY

Embedding Performance Assessments in All Courses

One way to maintain quality in your teacher education program is to require at least one project or task per course to be included in your students' portfolios. This gives all your students the opportunity to acquire—and document—skills and capabilities reflected in your program standards. We suggest the use of course-embedded assessments because they allow you to maintain quality in the portfolios that students produce. Your students cannot pass your teacher preparation courses without producing satisfactory performances and products and submitting documentation in their portfolios. When all members of your faculty are committed to requiring such projects or tasks that hold students to program standards, you can be reasonably sure that preservice teachers who are ready to graduate from your program have gained desired competencies and have created satisfactory portfolios. To prepare for this commitment, ask these questions:

1. What is the purpose of our students' portfolios?
2. Are we prepared to maintain standards by making sure that all students exit our courses with satisfactory course-embedded performance assessment projects or tasks?

Placing Performance Assessments on a Continuum

When determining the types of assessments to use in a course, it may help to visualize a continuum (see Figure 3.1.) On one end of the continuum there are assignments that assess discrete, discernible skills that can be evaluated alone. These may be used so that you can determine students' readiness to move on to a broader assignment, or to assess an important goal in depth. On the other end of the continuum there are assignments that reflect a wider range of abilities, which are used when you wish to survey the interaction of a variety of skills or to focus on the creation of a whole product. Projects or tasks can fall anywhere on this continuum, depending on their complexity, scope, and purpose.

As an example of using the continuum, suppose you want your students to write a lesson plan. You ask students to begin by writing a single lesson objective. You evaluate the students' objectives, return them, then ask them to begin writing an entire lesson plan. While the single objective assignment is focused on a very discrete

---

FIGURE 3.1   **A Continuum of Assessments for Courses in Higher Education**

Discrete Performances:
   Assessment Tasks

                                            Inclusive Performances:
                                               Assessment Projects

skill, it remains an authentic task, because the students later use it in lesson plans or units to be taught to groups of children. The lesson plan or unit is closer to the opposite end of the continuum, because it is a composite of a wider range of abilities. Thus, the continuum reflects the planning process for a course in a teacher preparation program.

It may become necessary to reexamine the types of work you are asking your students to do. We found this to be true in our work with performance assessments. Many of us are experienced professors who have held on to favorite assignments for years. We value authenticity and have come to realize that it also exists on a continuum (Cronin, 1993). However, we have found that we did not need to completely let go of assignments and projects that we had used successfully for a long time. By being realistic about the time constraints of a 15-week college semester, by taking advantage of resources available to us in our university library and in the elementary schools with which we have partnerships, and by taking less complex tasks into consideration, we could "move in a more authentic direction" (Cronin, 1993, p. 78) in our tasks and projects. When our assignments could be seen as authentic ones that have purpose, lead to real-life experiences, and contain an element of self-reflection, we have found that even the most discrete ones could be used as performance tasks that reflect genuine learning of a specific topic in a course (Meyer, 1992).

Choosing the types of assignments to be used for performance assessments in a course depends upon the nature of the course as well as the professor's teaching style and interest in assessing various types of abilities. These are the questions that can be asked as you choose the types of performance assessments to use:

1. How should course objectives be assessed?
2. Are there discrete skills that need to be evaluated in this course?
3. What are the time constraints that will need to be addressed if the students are to complete a performance assessment project, as opposed to smaller tasks?

Figures 3.2, 3.3, and 3.4 show examples of performance assessments that have worked well for us. These examples show the range of possibilities in the types of performances that you can require of students. Figure 3.2 shows a task that reflects the left end of the continuum, because it requires a discrete performance. This assignment is the time-on-task study that was mentioned previously. Figure 3.3 shows a project that reflects the right end of the continuum, because it requires inclusive performances. The project, the creation of a theme box, was also mentioned previously. It is the product of all learning in the course we call "Thematic Teaching"; thus, it actually controls the course. Figure 3.4 shows a performance assessment that is used in our course called "Language and Literacy." It falls in the middle of the continuum, because it is a project that reflects several standards and objectives; however, because of the broad nature of the content taught in this course, it is not the sole product of the course. Each of these figures includes the description of the project or task, the standard or standards that it meets, and some behavioral indicators or performance criteria associated with it.

Getting Projects or Tasks Ready for the Portfolio

Once projects or tasks are satisfactorily completed as class assignments, we ask our students to insert them into their portfolios. Three parts for each entry are to be inserted in the portfolio:

1. *Artifact:* This is the actual work produced by completing the assignment. It may comprise a written paper, teaching materials, a videotape, photographs, or any physical evidence of the work that has been done.
2. *Self-reflection statement:* Students are required to write a short statement that describes how this project or task added to their own learning of the subject.
3. *Portfolio cover sheet:* Before inserting this document in the portfolio under a particular standard, the student must summarize it with a cover sheet. This sheet contains a rationale, which explains how the document reflects knowledge of the standard, as well as how the assignment helped the student grow professionally.

FIGURE 3.2   Time-on-Task Performance Assessment Task

**Performance Assessment Task for Instructional Strategies:
A Time-on-Task Study**

Description

Students in the Instructional Strategies course are required to do a 1-hour observation in which they observe at least one entire lesson; for example, students might observe a math class or a language arts block. The focus of this observation is the behavior and engagements of two children as the lesson progresses. Students ask the classroom teacher if there are particular children whom they would like to have observed. Otherwise, the college student chooses two at random to observe. A specified format for the observation report is followed. In the report the children are kept anonymous. Data on each task that occurs during the lesson and each change of behavior in the two students are recorded. After presenting the data, students write a summary of their observations, a description of the possible implications for academic learning, and hypotheses for strategies that would increase the academic learning time of these two students. They conclude their reports with reflections on what they learned. As this is a required portfolio document, a cover sheet is also needed. The goal for this task is that preservice teachers become aware of the implications of time on task for academic learning time and understand the value of systematically observing how students engage in learning.

Standard Addressed

Standard #5, Classroom Motivation and Management Skills

Behavioral Indicators:

1. The students will collect data on the way individual children spend class time.
2. The students will objectively summarize time-on-task data.
3. The students will draw appropriate inferences about specific children's academic learning time.
4. The students will hypothesize appropriate strategies for increasing the time on task of individual children.
5. The students will verbalize a strong value for maximizing academic learning time in their classrooms.

FIGURE 3.3   **Theme Box Performance Assessment Project**

**Performance Assessment Project for Thematic Teaching in Early
Childhood: Building an Integrated, Thematic Curriculum**

Description

Working in small groups, students enrolled in Thematic Teaching in Early
Childhood construct interdisciplinary thematic resource units. Each group
of students chooses a theme focus and develops an entire resource collection
around that topic. The students' efforts are mainly devoted to creating a theme
resource guide. The guide contains several parts: (1) core concepts or general
understandings, (2) background information reports, (3) integrated activity
ideas, (4) graphic organizers, (5) resource bibliographies, (6) a glossary, and
(7) performance assessments. In addition, students design and construct
materials that address the concepts. They select and order high-quality
children's literature and teacher resources appropriate to the theme. The final
product of each team, a "theme box," is circulated as a resource to teachers and
student teachers through the university library.

Standards Addressed

Standard #1, Knowledge of Subject Matter

Behavioral Indicators:

1. The students will identify the key global concepts or general
   understandings for their themes.
2. The students will write accurate, in-depth information reports on their
   topics.
3. The students will evaluate and select resources and children's literature
   that address subject matter in a comprehensive and accurate manner.
4. The students will organize and annotate bibliographies of appropriate
   sources for their topics.

Standard #4, Multiple Instructional Strategies

Behavioral Indicators:

1. The students will use a wide repertoire of teaching models in their
   integrated activity ideas.
2. The students will design learning activities that enable children to
   construct their own learning.

FIGURE 3.3 *Continued*

3. The students will design learning experiences that build on children's life experiences, prior knowledge, and interests.

4. The students will design teaching materials and technology that will increase children's understanding of the concepts.

Standard #7, Instructional Planning Skills

Behavioral Indicators:

1. The students will organize a resource unit that ensures children will develop an in-depth understanding of the global concepts.

2. The students will generate activities that enable learners to see connections across subject matter areas.

3. The students will utilize community resources in their thematic units.

4. The students will relate activities and materials to core concepts and learning goals.

Standard #8, Assessment of Student Learning

Behavioral Indicator:

1. The students will design performance assessments that synthesize the content of their theme study and address the core concepts.

FIGURE 3.4   **Directed Reading Thinking Activity**

Performance Assessment Project for Language and Literacy: Exploring the DRTA

Description

One of the most generalizable and useful teaching strategies that a teacher of reading can use is the Directed Reading Thinking Activity (DRTA). This project enables students to thoroughly understand this strategy by researching it, observing it, planning for it, and actually teaching it. Students observe a designated teacher, who models his or her teaching of the DRTA with elementary students; they then write a thank-you letter to the teacher, explaining specifically what they learned during the observation. They also observe a lesson that the professor models in class and read handouts and textbook materials associated with it. Then students choose a part of the DRTA that is most interesting or puzzling to them and research the theoretical premise of this aspect of the DRTA. They write a brief summary of the information found in a source other than the course textbook. Next they write a DRTA plan, using a literature selection from a list of choices and following handout guides. Finally they teach the lesson they have planned to any number of students that suits their current situation and background experience, and they seek feedback from a professional other than the professor. They submit all reports and the lesson plan once for a grade and feedback, then resubmit them for process points after revisions are made. Use of technology is required for obtaining research or implementing parts of the lesson plan. To document this project, students need to include all reports, the lesson plan, work samples from the children, photographs of the lesson, a self-reflective statement within the body of the report, peer and professional feedback forms, and a cover sheet with a rationale for their portfolio.

Standards Addressed

Standard #4, Multiple Instructional Strategies

Behavioral Indicators:

1. The students will research the theoretical premise behind an instructional strategy.

2. The students will recognize the strategy when observing in a classroom.

3. The students will demonstrate understanding of the purpose of a specific instructional strategy by teaching it for this purpose.

FIGURE 3.4 *Continued*

Standard #7, Lesson Planning

Behavioral Indicators:

1. The students will plan a lesson that utilizes a variety of strategies.

2. The students will demonstrate appropriate teaching decisions for the use of instructional strategies in a variety of situations.

3. The students will self-reflect and articulate their own understanding of professional growth after teaching a lesson.

4. The students will write lesson plans that set clear purposes or objectives, show appropriate progression of activities and strategies for meeting those purposes or objectives, and allow for assessment and evaluation of children's attainment of objectives.

5. The students will make instructional decisions about the types of materials to use in a lesson and demonstrate understanding of active involvement in their learning by choosing materials accordingly.

6. The students will demonstrate understanding of the importance of making detailed written lesson plans as beginning preservice teachers.

HOW RUBRICS MAINTAIN QUALITY

As our students complete their performance assessments and insert them into their portfolios, they need to know what we expect of them. Naturally, the course professor sets criteria for projects or tasks in each individual course. But we also wanted students to know how we would view their work when it becomes part of the whole picture of their learning—the portfolio. Program-wide rubrics became necessary, so that we could help students maintain the quality of their portfolios.

According to Farr and Tone (1994), the scoring scale of a rubric must reflect "the intended uses of the assessment" (p. 220). We recommend that a portfolio system be designed in such a way that your faculty can help students set goals, gain control over their learning, and showcase their strengths. Rubrics can help your students understand the purpose of the portfolio system and guide them in meeting the criteria that you expect of them. These rubrics also guide your faculty and generate reliability during checkpoint conferences.

Working together to develop these rubrics is important. Faculty and student feedback on the numbers, terms, and conditions outlined in rubrics can help develop them into mutually agreed upon standards of evaluation.

Features of Rubrics

Because there is such a large variance of work in students' portfolios, we suggest using a three-point scale of "exceptional," "acceptable," and "not acceptable." While this scale is not sensitive enough to distinguish minute details of the portfolios, it is intended to be a general guideline and a broad set of expectations. Within the scale two factors can be taken into consideration: quantity of documents and overall quality of the connection of documents to standards.

1. *Quantity of documents.* As we explain in more detail in Chapter 4, we suggest that your faculty establish some checkpoints at which students will conference with an advisor about their portfolios. Rubrics can help guide these checkpoint conferences because they contain criteria for the number of documents

expected in the portfolio at each of the checkpoints. These criteria reflect the number of courses and types of experiences that a typical student would have had at each point. By the final checkpoint, students whose portfolios are acceptable would have documented all standards. Appendix C shows three rubrics that we use, one for each academic year that the students are in our program.

2. *Quality of the connection of documents to standards.* The rubrics are designed to establish how well the performances and products of students are connected to standards and refined as evidence for reviewers. Qualities to look for are:

a. Demonstration of the adopted standards

b. Appropriate use of rationales

c. Evidence of reflection

d. Absence of mechanical errors

e. Reflection of the age range of children for which the preservice teacher will be certified

f. Professional and visually appealing appearance

Each of the levels on your scale would reflect the degrees of existence that you feel are necessary for a particular rating. As can be seen in the rubrics in Appendix C, it is important to include "parallelism" (Farr & Tone, 1994), in that each level on the scale contains one of the listed criteria, with distinguishing adjectives, terms, or considerations to differentiate "exceptional," "acceptable," and "not acceptable" ratings from each other.

How Portfolio Rubrics Guide Student Work

An additional assurance that students will maintain ownership of their portfolios is to require them to submit different types of documents, with differing purposes. Thus, in our rubrics we delineate three types of documents to be included in the students' portfolios: course-embedded performance assessment tasks or projects, self-selected documents, and self-generated documents. All of these document types reflect different kinds of learning, as well as different degrees of self-motivation. They are described in the following subsections, and an explanation is given of their importance in determining the rating category of a student's portfolio.

Performance Assessment Projects or Tasks

This type of document, which is described in detail earlier in this chapter, is course-embedded. It is assigned by the course professor and is a synthesis of at least some of the course content. In order for it to be a meaningful portfolio document, the course professor requires a rationale to be submitted with this assignment.

Performance assessments are evidence of the kinds of learning that you value. In our program we require these projects or tasks in each course that we teach, so a student's working portfolio will contain more than a dozen completed and graded performance assessments at the end of his or her college career. This gives a picture of the student as an emerging professional, as well as of our program. Therefore, making sure that performance assessments are course-embedded is extremely important in a program-wide effort to ensure overall quality in students' portfolios.

Self-Selected Documents

The self-selected document is an assignment from any college credit course that the student selects to put in the portfolio. Unlike performance assessment projects, this type of assignment is not required by the course professor to be added to a portfolio; instead, the student chooses to include it as documentation of one of the standards. As with all documents that are entered into the student's portfolio, the student must create a cover sheet and write a rationale for the document.

This type of document is also important in the overall quality of a student's portfolio, because it shows what the student views as valuable. It reflects the student's decision-making and self-reflection, in terms of how he or she views personal and professional growth. One of our professors uses a simple exercise that evokes an internal dialogue about an artifact and proposed standard. Students can invite a peer to assist in decision making about including the item in the portfolio. This exercise is shown in Figure 3.5.

FIGURE 3.5 Example of a Self-Reflection Exercise in Selecting Documents for the Portfolio

Artifact and Standard Selection

1. Select an artifact for your portfolio.
2. Mentally review the activity and reflect upon the process and product. Reflect on the greatest value of this activity or experience. Connect that value to one of the ten standards.
3. Write a rationale about your selection.
4. Be sure to explain the following and include it in your portfolio with the artifact:
   a. Why I chose this piece
   b. What I learned and the competence I gained
   c. My future goals

During a portfolio checkpoint interview in our department, advisors check for the number of these documents included in the portfolio as well as the reflectiveness of the rationale, according to criteria established in the rubric. The quality of the specific document would already have been determined by the individual instructor when the student took the course.

Self-Generated Documents
When a student creates an artifact to document professional growth achieved outside of class and not assessed by an instructor, the resulting document is called self-generated. This type of document could represent attendance at professional conferences, independent readings, nonrequired work done in classrooms, participation in cultural events, and volunteer work. The student also needs to create a cover sheet and write a rationale for the document.

Because of the personal initiative required to create self-generated documents, they say much about the student's motivation to grow professionally and continue to learn outside of class. During portfolio conferences the quantity of these documents, as well as the substance of the rationale, needs to be checked by an advisor.

The Evolving Nature of Rubrics

The success of a portfolio system depends largely on the ability of the rubrics to perform their function. They must accurately reflect agreed-upon criteria for portfolios, yet they must also serve as a guide for goal setting and personal reflection. We have found that our rubrics should be flexible; indeed, ours have been revised several times to meet the approval of our faculty and the needs of our students. We provide all incoming students with copies of these rubrics so that they know well in advance how to prepare their portfolios and what is expected of them.

CONCLUSION

The key to cultivating outstanding teaching and learning through the use of portfolios is the use of course-embedded performance assessments. When faculty members agree to require these projects or tasks in each course in the teacher education program, students' portfolios show that they are capable of demonstrating the knowledge, skills, and dispositions that it takes to be a teacher. Other types of portfolio documents add to this by showing the students' interests and initiatives outside their required courses. Thus, through the presentation of performance assessments or tasks, self-selected documents, and self-generated artifacts following a program rubric, portfolios will be more than just pretty scrapbooks.

Chapter 4 will show how quality of student learning is maintained and assessed in a formative way. A program-wide effort to support students as they create their portfolios is described.

► 4

Supporting Students
As They Document
Their Learning

WHY A SUPPORT SYSTEM IS NECESSARY

When we began requiring performance assessments and students started to develop their portfolios, we were pleasantly surprised at their enthusiasm. After all, documenting all the work done in their teacher preparation program is no easy task, and we marveled at their inclination to embrace this work. We soon came to realize, however, that their motivation was driven by pragmatism; our students saw their portfolios as vehicles for getting a job after graduation. In a tight job market they were eager to find an "edge" over other candidates. Thus, they were excited about the prospect of using portfolios as interviewing tools and willingly put themselves to work at creating attractive—and thick—notebooks that showcased their teaching abilities.

While this excitement was welcome, we once again reexamined the perception that our students had of portfolios. We were worried that our students would be driven by the mere creation of an end product, rather than by the self-reflection of learning and the setting of professional and academic goals. It was not enough to simply mandate the creation of professional portfolios, even with a set of well-written guidelines. Doing this would only produce a smattering of attractive scrapbooks done by the most self-disciplined students. To have a comprehensive assessment system, we needed to be formative in our evaluation of preservice teachers.

One of the teacher behaviors that we talk about often in our courses is "facilitation." Because our department's philosophy is constructivist, this is an important behavior, because it is the mode through which teachers guide their students in their learning. We decided that it was vitally important to the success of the program for us to do just that for our students—facilitate their learning and professional growth. Thus, we began a system of support during the process of building portfolios. Because the portfolio system was designed to help our students become self-reflective as they met a set of standards, they needed more than just a textbook to follow when developing their portfolios. They needed committed and interested faculty members who were involved in each step of their portfolio development. They needed to see a reason for completing portfolios other than as a means to an employment end. They needed to see the value of self-reflection, goal setting, peer collaboration, and partnerships with practitioners.

We feel that a portfolio assessment system that gives students frequent opportunities to observe models, discuss goals and successes with others, and evaluate themselves continuously facilitates a true learning experience for all of us. This requires a program-wide support system.

WHAT IS NEEDED FOR SUPPORT

We suggest a support system for portfolio development that consists of three entities: mentor/peer support, partnership schools or a professional development school (PDS), and conferencing checkpoints. In our program, mentor or peer support offers students the opportunity to stay in touch with a peer or mentor who is familiar with the requirements of the program or course. Our PDS provides our preservice teachers with a context outside the university classroom that is consistent with our philosophy and our valuing of portfolios.

Conferencing checkpoints in our program give students set times for reflection and sharing of learning. These necessary components of a successful portfolio system are explained in the following pages.

Mentor/Peer Support: Staying in Touch

In your teacher education program you can offer students two ways of collaborating with and supporting each other as they learn and grow professionally. The first method, mentoring, is a program-wide effort. The second method, peer support, can be done in individual classrooms, but is most effective when all professors of individual courses implement such support. Both are described in this section.

Mentoring in the Teacher Education Program

Mentoring is an effective way to initiate and facilitate the academic growth of freshmen at your university who have indicated an interest in becoming teachers. In our program, mentors are selected from honor students in the department, especially from the membership of Kappa Delta Pi, an honor society in education. Mentors are charged with the responsibility of being sources of information and guidance, providing moral support, and serving as role models. Our mentors and their protégés are introduced at a freshman orientation meeting, and they stay in touch throughout the year through scheduled luncheons and e-mail. Each mentor is also asked to attend one or more university-wide events, such as Freshman Move-in Day, Family Day during Homecoming Weekend, or the annual phone-athon.

From their mentors, freshmen learn early on about the goals, policies, and procedures of the department. During their first semester on campus, students have the opportunity to see their mentors' portfolios. Well in advance of enrolling in their first education class and receiving formal preparation in portfolio development, freshmen become aware of the value of saving important assignments and carefully documenting all fieldwork. The mentoring program is an important way to motivate students toward meaningful learning from the beginning of their college careers.

Peer Support in the College Classroom

The concept of receiving support from peers can be used in individual college classrooms. You can refer students who are in need of support to students who have already completed your course or similar courses. The way one of our professors accomplishes this is by establishing a relationship with the Writing Center and the Tutoring Center on our campus, two widely used student services. The professor meets with the director of each of these centers, explaining the concept of portfolios and the use of rationales, as well as the performance assessment project required for the class. In addition, handouts that give detailed descriptions and models of the project are passed along. Thus, people who work at the Writing Center and Tutoring Center are aware of the types of assignments that this course requires, so that they can be of more help when working with students. In addition, this professor requests an elementary education major (preferably one who has already completed the class) to tutor or provide assistance to the students when they are asked to go to one of the service centers, so that it can be reasonably certain that the tutor is familiar with terms such as "cover sheet," "rationale," "performance assessment," and so forth. This type of support has been particularly helpful to students in the class who struggle with articulating their self-reflection of learning.

Peer editing is another way that you can provide peer support within the college classroom. This is an important part of the process of completing the performance assessment task, because it requires your students to make sure that their work clearly articulates their understanding for an audience other than the professor. This concept not only helps students improve their work, but it also models the real-life work of professionals. In our classes, peer editors can be assigned or chosen, but they are always recommended when producing documents for the portfolio. Figures 4.1 and 4.2 show some peer editing forms that some of us like to use. Figure 4.1 shows a general form that can be used with performance assessment projects or tasks. The form shown in Figure 4.2 is particularly helpful for use in the entry-level course in which students learn how to write rationales for their portfolio cover sheets.

FIGURE 4.1   Example of a Peer Editing Form to Be Used with Performance Assessments

Peer Editor Reaction Sheet

Author's name: _____   Author's SS#: _____

Editor's SS#: _____

General reaction after first reading:

Specific comments after second reading:

Perceived strengths (+):

Apparent weaknesses (–):

Tentative suggestions (?):

Overall rating on this draft:

_____ Professional paper—Ready for portfolio

_____ Draft—Still needs some work

Directions for Peer Editing:

  Use Social Security numbers to identify editors. You may have only the time between two class periods to review and edit. Peer editors need to make summary comments on the evaluation sheet and also mark places on the draft that need correction. When using more than one peer editor, each editor should use a different colored pen and put his or her Social Security number on the paper. Authors have final accountability for any changes made to the paper.

Continued

FIGURE 4.1   *Continued*

Below are the criteria to evaluate:

A. General Content

1. Presentation is clear.
2. Organization is logical.
3. The paper is interesting to read.
4. The length is appropriate.
5. Both a summary and a personal reaction are included.
6. Author uses his or her own words.
7. Author uses appropriate resources.

B. Mechanics: Typical Problems

1. Incomplete sentences
2. Run-on sentences
3. Awkward wording or incorrect word choice
4. Changing tense
5. Apostrophe use
6. Spelling
7. Typographical errors

One last recommendation for providing peer support is what we call "Portfolio Day." This is a day when students who are student teaching are excused from their elementary classroom duties and revisit the college campus, portfolios in hand. Because they are almost finished working on their portfolios, they have a wealth of information and advice to offer sophomores and juniors who are just getting started. Professors invite the student teachers into their classrooms to talk about their portfolios. They show their peers what they have completed thus far and talk about what they have left to do. Students illustrate how the portfolio is used for instructional planning, self-reflecting, setting goals, and monitoring professional opportunities, as well as how they are using it as a teaching tool in the classroom. They offer advice about saving documents and writing rationales. Students enrolled in methods classes are usually interested in learning about what to expect in their own upcoming student teaching experience; therefore, the presenters show them artifacts that reflect the work they have done in classrooms. We have found this to be an extremely valuable way to have students connect with each other.

FIGURE 4.2   Example of a Peer Editing Form to Be Used When Reading Portfolio Cover Sheets

Peer Editing for a Portfolio Cover Sheet

Name of author: _____

Name of editor: _____

Date: _____

Read the entire cover sheet once. Respond to these questions during the second reading.

A. Heading

    1. Were a standard number and title given? _____

    2. Does the use of this particular standard make good sense to you? _____ (If not, discuss this with the author.)

    3. In what way could the title given to this document be improved? [Hint: Often titles include artifact names given in the glossary in Chapter 4 of *How to Develop a Professional Portfolio* (Campbell et al., 1997).]

_____

    4. Were a date and course designation (if appropriate) given? _____

B. Rationale

    1. Description of the document:

       Does the paragraph start by explaining exactly what the document itself is? _____

       Does it explain the experience behind the document? _____

       How can this explanation be improved to be more clear or complete?

_____

    2. Reflection

       Does the paragraph address how this experience improved competence or how the document is an indicator of professional growth? _____

       Does the reflection integrate this work with prior knowledge or beliefs? _____

       Does the reflection show focus and logic? _____

       Does the reflection indicate new insights that can be applied in the future? _____

The student teachers benefit because they have a chance to showcase valued work, practice articulating their own learning, and receive affirmation about their accomplishments as beginning teachers. The students in our methods classes benefit because they receive some very practical suggestions for creating and using portfolios and have an opportunity to interact with some very real role models.

The Professional Development School: Providing Authenticity

Supporting students as they grapple with educational theory and its implications for their work in the classroom is a vital part of our program. We have found that it is necessary to provide students with a clinical site for testing theory-based curricular practices. Thus, in 1995, we strengthened our partnership with a local elementary school and formed our Professional Development School. This setting is not just a place where students in field classes and student teachers go to fulfill their certification requirements, but it is a place where students witness collaboration between the school and the university. It is a place where students see a model of continuous learning that fosters the professional growth of teachers and university faculty, and a place where research is translated into practice and practice is connected to research. Programs hosted at our PDS include practicum and student teaching programs, field experiences, an undergraduate methods class, and one graduate curriculum class. School faculty and administrators participate in team teaching and assist in the planning of practical application of theory, while one teacher serves as an adjunct faculty member within our department. Each of these programs focuses on delivering content and includes performance assessment tasks or projects that are to be inserted in students' portfolios.

The PDS is important to our growth as a program in many ways. According to the National Commission on Teaching and America's Future (1996), PDS can help ensure high-quality teacher preparation. However, one of the best reasons to maintain this partnership is the fact that professors in our program and elementary school teachers become true team members in helping our students learn. Teachers at the PDS who view teaching through the constructivist philosophy become our colleagues in helping our students understand its classroom implications. This is truly a support system for our students, who seek active construction of their own knowledge of pedagogy and who need to internalize the value of portfolios. The PDS is a place where teachers also value the use of portfolios in their own classrooms, as well as in designing their own professional growth. Therefore, through the PDS, our students have a rich environment in which they can witness inservice teachers and administrators using the portfolio in a variety of ways (ways they might not otherwise see): assisting in hiring new teachers and administrators, mentoring beginning teachers, selecting substitute teachers, documenting program development, securing grants and funding, enhancing instruction, expanding teacher evaluation through national certification standards, documenting standards for school accreditation, and creating portfolios that showcase partnerships and community work. Figure 4.3 shows an example of one way that our students can witness portfolio development by an inservice teacher.

Thus, a PDS can create "opportunities for learning by teaching, learning by doing, and learning by collaborating" in your teacher education program (Darling-Hammond, 1994, p. 10). When a program can enhance "the learning of teacher educators and veteran teachers as well as beginning teachers" (p. 10), it offers a strong scaffold of support for its preservice students.

Conferencing Checkpoints: Maintaining Contact

Checkpoints are times for students to stop and reassess what they are doing. Such times can be built into your teacher education program, so that students can discuss portfolio or performance assessment work with a professor, reflect on their learning, and set goals.

In order to maintain an understanding of your program goals and to facilitate attainment of standards, we contend that you will need a system of checkpoints for your students. There are three

---

FIGURE 4.3   A Model of Portfolio Development by a Teacher at the PDS

Cathy Hayden is a veteran PDS teacher with 27 years of experience. She regularly shares her own portfolio with our students when they visit her classroom as well as when she lectures at the university. In her portfolio our students see documentation of action research, projects, application of technology, parent–teacher exchanges, experiences with student support services, and participation in staff development. While this portfolio is important for our students to see, the process has also helped Mrs. Hayden continue to grow, making her a model of professionalism for our teachers. She shares her insights:

> Along with our district supervisor of Curriculum and Instruction and several of my fellow teachers, I attended a full day workshop on development, maintenance, and utilization of portfolios in the elementary classroom. I had used children's portfolios in my classes for nearly my entire teaching career, but at the start the portfolio contained just collections of student work that I chose. Over time, the portfolios in my classroom became a true holistic picture of a child: interests, strengths, and needs. My third graders expressed pride in their portfolios, shared their work with others and developed goals for increased improvement. As I continued to refine the concept of portfolios in my classroom, portfolios became a crucial component in the evaluation and celebration of student achievement. As a result of the value gleaned from having students develop control and responsibility for their growth, I saw that the true power of the portfolio was in self-reflection. So as you can see, this workshop was just a continued part of my study in the use of portfolios in my classroom.
>
> As we listened to the portfolio workshop presenters, I smiled with agreement as philosophy and procedures were discussed. I jotted down notes on unique ways to store portfolios and added a new student reading survey to my workshop folder. At one point during the presentation, our district supervisor looked down at the table, and said, "Cathy, you should make a portfolio." I smiled and agreed. However, as the workshop continued, I thought, "Developing a portfolio is a lot of work! Too much work!"
>
> About two or three weeks later, the university coordinator for our PDS was in my classroom to observe my student teacher. As my student teacher prepared for her lesson, the coordinator leaned over and whispered, "Oh, I understand you're considering making a portfolio. This will be a wonderful example to share with our university students." After recovering from my surprise, I very quickly explained that although making a portfolio would be interesting, it was definitely too much work for me. She smiled as we turned our attention to the start of the student teacher's lesson.
>
> A month or so later following a teachers' meeting, the district supervisor said, "Cathy, I was talking to the university PDS coordinator about your making a portfolio and we thought what a valuable resource it would be for our partnership." I explained that although I agreed as to the value of the portfolio, it was just too much work. I thought she

FIGURE 4.3 *Continued*

seemed somewhat disappointed, but I wasn't quite convinced that the issue was defeated. I decided to be more proactive and clear up any misconceptions that they might have about my making a professional portfolio. You see, my negative responses to their inquiries probably carried mixed messages because I truly believe in the value of portfolios. Yet I wanted to politely say "no."

After explaining my situation to my husband, he asked why the administration and the university would want me to make a portfolio. I explained its use as a model for student teachers and other university students. He asked if the university students were using their portfolios to acquire a job. I explained that this was true, but went on to explain that the true power of the portfolio is its self-reflective component. As we continued to talk about the value of the portfolio in developing goals and documenting successes, I stopped and looked sternly at my husband and said, "You know, I have now talked myself into making a professional portfolio!" And so I did.

And yes, it was a lot of work, but I did find its real value to me was in the self-reflection I used in constructing it and am continuing to use as I maintain it. So it has added to my growth as a teacher. My portfolio has helped me make a strong connection with the university students with whom I have the opportunity to share it. I see myself better equipped to help my student teachers develop and strengthen their portfolios. The insights I gained from developing my portfolio have impacted my third graders as well. I always share my portfolio with my classes. My portfolio is a model for my students as their portfolios take on greater importance to them. I see improved student portfolios in their content and presentation, and in the attention students devote to the portfolio creation, maintenance, and sharing.

I first made this professional portfolio during my twenty-fifth year as an elementary teacher. For me, making my portfolio was and continues to be an exciting, rewarding experience!

Used with permission of Cathy Hayden.

purposes for each checkpoint: (1) to ascertain that program requirements are being met, (2) to have students present and discuss their portfolios with a faculty advisor, and (3) to ensure a growing understanding of the program philosophy. In our program, passing or failing any checkpoint is unrelated to passing courses; a student who fails to meet some of the criteria for the checkpoint is merely flagged for further monitoring. A student who fails to pass any checkpoint leaves the conference knowing exactly why. A plan for improvement is written and the student must initiate another conference with the advisor or instructor at a later date. We provide a supportive approach to portfolio work that focuses on continuous improvement and goal setting for all students, especially for those experiencing difficulty.

We suggest that the timing of the checkpoints coincide roughly with the sophomore, junior, and senior academic years of the students' college careers. Each of our checkpoints are briefly explained in the next few pages.

Sophomore-Level Checkpoint

During the entry-level course to the teacher preparation program the sophomore-level checkpoint can take place. The philosophy that your program has adopted can be introduced and explained during this course, with ongoing referrals to it as students connect the philosophy to their academic and/or fieldwork. Students can be introduced to the process of portfolio assessment and begin creating their portfolios. They can learn the skill of writing rationales that are inserted on cover sheets for each document that they wish to put in the portfolio. They can view the portfolios of others, such as student teachers who are preparing to graduate as well as practicing teachers and faculty members. They can also be shown the idea of self-reflection and its importance in their learning as well as in their documentation of program standards.

By the end of the semester in which our students take the entry-level course, they are asked to present at least three artifacts with cover sheets. This is outlined in a rubric that is given to the students when they enter the program and defines the criteria needed for acceptable portfolios (see Appendix C). They participate in a conference during the last week of the semester. This can be an individual or group interview, in which the course professor evaluates the portfolio according to the designated rubric. The professor as well as fellow students assist with goal setting for future portfolio work, check for understanding of the departmental philosophy, and monitor progress in meeting department and college requirements. Feedback from the professor and classmates centers around four questions:

1. Is the portfolio itself well organized, professional-looking, and visually appealing?

2. Do the artifacts appropriately document attainment of skills and knowledge in the corresponding standard?

3. Do the documents provide compelling evidence of professional growth and competence? Have the documents been revised based on any constructive criticism from professors?

4. Do the rationales clearly explain the documents and establish their value? Have the rationales been revised and edited based on prior recommendations from peer editors and the course professor?

Figure 4.4 shows a set of guidelines for a small group conference at this checkpoint. Figure 4.5 shows the "Checkpoint Evaluation Form" that is completed by professors who teach the Instructional Strategies course and is filed in the student's permanent record.

Junior-Level Checkpoint

The second checkpoint can be scheduled for the junior academic year. We recommend that this checkpoint involve individual conferences that can help your students help themselves, so that they are aware of what they have learned thus far, what they value in teaching, and what they have yet to learn. While holding them to standards of quality is vitally important, the purpose is not to evaluate as much as it is to facilitate academic and professional growth. Because this checkpoint is not connected to a particular course, a conference can take place with any faculty member who has a compatible schedule. This advisor has the responsibility of making certain that the student is meeting program requirements, understanding the department's philosophy, and documenting standards appropriately in his or her portfolio. We ask our faculty advisors to set aside 1 hour per week for interviews; usually the time actually needed is far less than that.

One of the purposes of this type of portfolio system is to allow students to gain some autonomy over their learning. Thus, we suggest that, prior to the conference, students be required to complete and submit a self-assessment exercise for the purpose of setting academic or professional goals. This exercise requires that students reflect upon their understanding of the standards that their teacher

FIGURE 4.4   Sophomore-Level Group Conferencing Guidelines

Sophomore-Level Checkpoint Conferences: Instructions for Small Groups

Today you have the opportunity to share your beginning portfolio with a small group of classmates. We will be using this format for your sharing time:

1. Sharing Reactions (5 minutes)

We'll begin by asking everyone to briefly comment on what portfolio development has been like for you. What has surprised you, frustrated you, or excited you?

2. Sharing Documents (15–20 minutes)

Having discussed these general feelings about portfolio development, each of you will now present your selection of portfolio documents. In order to receive feedback from peers on the presentation of your portfolio, you should ask your classmates questions like these:

"What clarification, if any, do I need to make on what these documents are and the work or experiences they represent?"

"To what extent have I convinced you of the value of these experiences and documents to my professional growth?"

"Have I chosen appropriate standards for filing the documents?"

"Did I make a visual impact with my portfolio?"

You should feel free to solicit any additional feedback on any portfolio entry.

3. Sharing Ideas for Future Documents (15–20 minutes)

By now you no doubt have several ideas for possible future documents from seeing the portfolios of your classmates. This is the time to ask for the help of your peers and Instructional Strategies professor in deciding issues like how best to document a valuable out-of-class experience, what to do about a very large or cumbersome original work, or what standard relates best to a particular experience. Perhaps you have questions about good ways to document a particular standard or how to achieve a balance of types of artifacts.

4. Sharing Goals (10 minutes)

You were asked to come to this interview having given advance thought to some personal goals for continued professional development. After having this portfolio sharing time, you may wish to amend those goals and/or add goals to your list. We will take a few quiet moments for you to make changes to your goal list and to record your revised goals statements on the Sophomore Checkpoint Evaluation Form, which will stay in your folder. Then you will each share with the group at least one of your goals for portfolio development and continued professional growth.

5. Sign Off (5 minutes)

In concluding the interview, I will complete the Sophomore Checkpoint Evaluation Form that will be retained in your folder in the department office. Congratulations! Your portfolio is well under way, and, more importantly, the professional growth it represents has begun.

FIGURE 4.5   Evaluation Form Used at the Sophomore Checkpoint in the Instructional Strategies Class

**Instructional Strategies Interview Evaluation Form:
Checkpoint #1**

Name _____ SS# _____

Date of Interview _____ Name of Interviewer _____

1. Student's Portfolio Interview:

    (This section is completed by the interviewer.)

    _____ Student's portfolio met exceptional level.

    _____ Student's portfolio met acceptable level.

    _____ Student's portfolio did not meet the acceptable level.

2. Student's Knowledge of the Constructivist Model:

    (This section is completed by the interviewer.)

    _____ Student answered the constructivist questions appropriately.

    _____ Student needs greater understanding of constructivism.

3. Checkpoint #1 Program Requirements:

    (This section is completed by the Elementary/Early Childhood Education Office.)

    _____ Student has completed all the program requirements for Checkpoint #1.

    _____ Student has been placed on hold for Checkpoint #1 for the following reasons:

    _____

    _____

_____ Student *met* all three requirements for Checkpoint #1.

_____ Student *did not meet* all three requirements for Checkpoint #1.

Interviewer's Signature: _____

Note: Faculty member and student should record plans for improvement and goals for continued development on the back of this form.

education program has adopted and the kinds of teacher behaviors that exemplify these standards. To do this in our program, each student is given a set of forty-five cards that contain descriptions of teaching behaviors, skills, or dispositions. The student independently sorts these cards into ranked piles according to the kinds of skills or attitudes that he or she values. Appendix D shows directions and charts needed for completing the Self-Assessment Sorting Activity. After completing the sorting activity, the student completes a summary sheet that indicates the standards valued most. Based on these values, the student creates academic or professional goals and writes them on an application form. The summary sheet and the application are then submitted to the assigned faculty advisor prior to the conference. This gives the faculty advisor an opportunity to study the summary and the goals before the conference and, if necessary, make plans for guiding the student toward setting additional academic and professional goals.

Making sure that your students know the theoretical orientation and practical implications of the philosophy you espouse is another part of this interview. Students should be prepared to answer at least one question about this philosophy, in which theory as well as practice is addressed. Examples of questions that may be asked are:

1. How would you define this philosophy for a parent who is unfamiliar with it?
2. What is the role of the teacher in a classroom that reflects this philosophy?
3. How has your notion of this philosophy changed or developed in the last semester?
4. What philosophy of teaching and learning do you believe in? Do you have any documents in your portfolio to indicate that you are a teacher who believes in this philosophy? Which ones are they?
5. What part of this philosophy would you like to understand in more depth? How would you work on this?

Portfolio review and evaluation is another part of this conference, and probably its main point. Using a rubric that outlines what is necessary for inclusion in the portfolio helps to guide the interview. Appendix C shows an example of the rubric that we decided to use in our program. For their portfolios to be considered "acceptable," we ask our students to include one performance assessment from each course already taken by this point in our program, three self-selected documents, and three self-generated documents. Therefore, the interviewing advisor would simply look for these quantities, which can be done before the conference begins.

When considering the work in a student's portfolio during this checkpoint, the advisor evaluates only the self-generated documents and self-selected documents. This is because the course-embedded performance assessment tasks or projects have already been submitted for review by the professors who assigned them to their classes. Our students cannot pass courses without completing satisfactory performance assessment tasks or projects, so it can be reasonably assumed that their inclusion in the portfolio indicates their acceptable quality and their adherence to the criteria established for the task or project.

Other quality factors in the portfolio are also considered. The faculty advisor looks for rationales that clearly and concisely describe the document as well as its importance to the student's professional growth. Self-reflection is expected in the rationale and desired in the document itself. Overall professional appearance and editing are important, as is the inclusion of documentation of work with all age groups for which the student will be certified to teach.

When the advisor and the student sit down together to review the portfolio, their objective is to recognize the student's strengths, as shown in the quality of the self-generated and self-selected documents, and the standards that the student strongly values. Connections are made between what the student has accomplished up to this point and what the student believes is important for teachers to be able to do. The portfolio is a vehicle for professional growth because it is an ongoing, flexible representation of the student's abilities as well as a reflection of his or her values.

Areas of need are also recognized during the conference. If the student has not submitted an acceptable portfolio, the faculty advisor helps make plans for its revision. The student and advisor work together to write additional goals and make specific plans for meeting acceptable criteria. After the criteria have been met, the student must request another interview, with the same advisor, at a later date.

The pattern of documents included needs to be checked to determine that the student has included a variety of types of artifacts under a variety of standards. The Artifacts Checklist aids in this review, because it charts the course-embedded projects or tasks, self-selected documents, and self-generated documents that the student has included in the portfolio (see Appendix A). It gives everyone involved a clear picture of the types of assignments and experiences that have fostered the student's learning. Appendix E provides a transcript from a sample junior checkpoint conference.

Senior-Level Checkpoint

The last conferencing checkpoint in your program can take place during the students' senior year when they are student teaching. This checkpoint provides the opportunity for students to reflect upon their preservice training, assess their student teaching experiences, prepare for graduation, and showcase their accomplishments as they enter the teaching profession. Their portfolios, which have almost evolved into comprehensive presentation portfolios at this point, are a vehicle for organizing their classroom experience documentation, supporting reflective thinking, and monitoring their professional growth. We shall explain what has been done in our program to facilitate this checkpoint.

At the beginning of the senior year the students review grade-level and program options for their student teaching assignments. They are encouraged to explore these options with advisors and to select placements that meet their interests, goals, and area of certification. The student meets with the university supervisor and reviews his or her portfolio and student teaching requirements. The portfolio can help to guide the interview. For example, if it is determined that the student has few entries under Standard #9 (Professional Commitment and Responsibility), the university supervisor and the student discuss ways the student can gain experiences during student teaching (such as attending professional development activities, joining the state teachers' organization or learned societies, or attending conferences).

The student completes the "Professional Goals Worksheet" shown in Figure 4.6. Here, initial goals for student teaching are listed. The worksheet is placed in the student's portfolio and later shared along with the portfolio during the initial meeting with the supervising teacher and school principal. Some goals that have been written on student forms are also shown in Figure 4.6.

Students who will attend the PDS also submit to the university supervisor a 5-minute-long videotaped self-introduction that is used during the supervisor's placement meeting with the PDS building principal. The presentation includes a brief introductory statement including background information on the student's area of concentration. The student uses the portfolio to describe some of his or her most memorable preservice experiences and other selected activities. Finally, the student talks about goals and desired experiences for student teaching. This concept of using the portfolio as a way to assist in selecting appropriate cooperating teachers and programs for the student teacher came to us from our PDS elementary principal, who, as a partner with our teacher education program, was interested in finding practical ways to enhance the experiences that our students gained in her school.

During the semester prior to student teaching our students receive a letter notifying them that they will be required to bring their portfolios to the opening student teaching seminar. They are to come prepared to introduce themselves to their peers and the university supervisor through the use of their portfolios. Students are encouraged to select a variety of artifacts that present a complete portrait of themselves as preprofessionals. This experience encourages team building and provides a forum for students to prepare for their classroom presentations with the cooperating teachers and elementary students.

At the onset of his or her student teaching semester, the preservice teacher visits the assigned classroom and introduces himself or herself to the children and the cooperating teacher with the portfolio. A conference is also scheduled with the cooperating teacher, during which time the student presents the portfolio. During this

---

FIGURE 4.6   The Student Teaching Goal-Setting Form and Some Sample Student Teaching Goals

Professional Goals Worksheet

Name: _____ Date: _____

Directions:
List the goals you hope to accomplish during your student teaching experience.
(Duplicate this page if necessary for writing more than three goals.) At the end of the
student teaching experience, circle the level at which you have realized each goal and
comment on your experiences.

Goal #1: _____

Not Accomplished	Partially Accomplished	Mostly Accomplished	Entirely Accomplished
0 _____	1 _____	2 _____	3

Discussion:

Goal #2: _____

Not Accomplished	Partially Accomplished	Mostly Accomplished	Entirely Accomplished
0 _____	1 _____	2 _____	3

Discussion:

Goal #3: _____

Not Accomplished	Partially Accomplished	Mostly Accomplished	Entirely Accomplished
0 _____	1 _____	2 _____	3

Discussion:

FIGURE 4.6   *Continued*

"To expand my repertoire of teaching strategies to meet the needs of diverse learners (Standard #3)"

"To use a variety of assessment strategies, including performance assessments (Standard #8)"

"To develop strategies that promote higher order thinking (Standard #4)"

"To build relationships with parents and use community resources (Standard #10)"

"To expand my skills in classroom management and discipline (Standard #5)"

"To gain skill in the proper pacing of my lessons (Standard #7)"

conference, data are gathered by the cooperating teacher that assist the student to gain the skills and behaviors most needed. The value of this activity has been documented in responses from supervising teachers, administrators, and students. They report that using the portfolio personalizes the introduction, assists in organizing student teaching experiences around the program standards, and inspires children as well as teachers and administrators to maintain portfolios. All agree that using the portfolio as a means of introduction is more personal and meaningful than the one-page data sheet that is typical of programs without portfolios. As noted previously, it was a cooperating teacher at the PDS who suggested this idea to us—our partnership has given birth to many such creative and useful strategies.

Five formative assessments and one final evaluation are conducted throughout the student teaching experience. All of these assessments require the use of forms that are completed by cooperating teachers and university supervisors. We found that it was necessary to make sure that the forms coincided with the standards that we ask our students to meet by focusing on behavioral indicators of the standards. Revisions of old forms were guided by asking this question: "What performance criteria should a graduating senior demonstrate in the classroom, school, and community?" The congruency among the forms, checklists, evaluations, and standards has enabled our students' portfolios to become an integral part of the assessment and evaluation process.

The university supervisor conducts a series of formal observations throughout the student teaching experience. During the pre-observation and post-observation conferences the portfolio is examined for evidence of the behaviors that reflect the program standards. The student teacher prepares a statement of strengths, areas for improvement, and goals. These goals become the focus of future observations and conferences. The portfolio is a valuable resource because it serves as a basis for discussing the actual classroom practices of the student teacher as they are defined by the standards. It enables the student, the cooperating teacher, and the university supervisor to further validate the assessment with authentic experiences and personal examples. Incorporating the portfolio into conferences and evaluation enables the student teachers to assess their own work rather than rely solely on the supervisors' or cooperating teachers' assessment and evaluation. The student teaching process is no longer merely observer-based, but includes self-reflection and assessment by the students.

Our students are required to complete two student teaching assignments during their last 15-week semester. After 7 weeks in one classroom they move to another grade level for student teaching for the remaining weeks of the semester. Students are encouraged to collect additional artifacts that represent the standards during their student teaching experiences; however, many find it difficult to allocate time to enter artifacts into the portfolio and to generate rationales. We have suggested that they maintain folders, each labeled with a standard, and to file the artifacts until they can enter them into the portfolio.

We also recognize that in order for students to reflect upon their experiences, they must have time and support; thus, we reserve a few days between the two student teaching assignments for a variety of portfolio and assessment activities. During these "Portfolio Days," students organize the artifacts that they collected during their first student teaching assignment, construct rationales, work on the visual presentation of their portfolio, and establish goals for their second student teaching assignment. Supervisors ask them, "Is there anything that you have done over the past 7 weeks and during the last

3 days with your portfolio that suggests a change in the things you will do in your classroom during your next assignment?"

As previously discussed, these Portfolio Days also involve students visiting methods classes in the teacher education program at the university to present their portfolios to sophomores and juniors and offer advice about portfolio development and student teaching. Seniors explain the value of the portfolio to their student teaching experiences, describe appropriate artifacts, and model ways to use the portfolio. During some semesters a "Celebration Workshop" is conducted in which student teachers showcase their portfolios to the university community, representatives from local schools, and advisory board members.

During the final weeks of student teaching the reality of impending job searches becomes immediate, and student teachers work to ensure that their portfolios are balanced and their best work is displayed. Students examine and reexamine their artifacts and engage in mock interviews. Student teachers continue to refine their presentation portfolios.

An exit conference with the cooperating teacher and the student teacher is scheduled during the last week of student teaching. The goal of the session is to provide a forum in which the student teacher gains a clear understanding of his or her skills as a teacher and makes a transition from preservice to inservice status. Students are encouraged to summarize their most successful instructional activities drawn from the portfolio. This activity builds the student's confidence, provides evidence of growth in the knowledge of teaching, and illustrates how he or she has integrated the curriculum. The exit conference also provides an opportunity for the university supervisor to utilize the portfolio as a guide for discussing classroom practices and the teacher education curriculum with the supervising teacher. Should gaps or inadequacies in the program be identified, plans for new learning opportunities for future student teachers are created.

The senior exit interview is the final meeting between the student teacher and the university supervisor. The task of the first part of the interview is to confirm that all graduation and certification requirements have been met. The remainder of the discussion, which is structured as a collaborative dialogue, focuses on the student's portfolio. The rubric is used to measure the level of successful completion of the portfolio. As identified on the rubric, students who are at this point in their development are expected to have the following minimum requirements: performance assessments from each course in our program, six self-selected documents, and six self-generated documents, with at least one document entered for each standard (see Appendix C). As the portfolio is examined, the university supervisor asks the following questions:

1. At what level have you met your student teaching goals?
2. What goals will you take with you as a beginning teacher?
3. What are your plans for meeting those goals?
4. How will you use the portfolio as an inservice teacher?

We contend that use of the portfolio during the student teaching experience can strengthen your teacher preparation program, as it has ours. From the beginning to the end of the 15-week semester, portfolios can play a major role in the placement of student teachers, their introduction to cooperating teachers and children, their professional goal setting, and their preparation for the real world of teaching. Figure 4.7 shows some testimonials from professionals at our PDS, who discuss the benefits of incorporating portfolios in every part of the student teaching experience.

We concur with the research that suggests exposure to and use of portfolios in teacher education programs can play a critical role in positively influencing preservice teachers' beliefs and attitudes toward using portfolios (Ford & Ohlhausen, 1991; Mokhtari et al., 1996). In order to continue to improve our portfolio system, we ask students the following questions about the use of the portfolio during their preservice experience:

1. How has the development of this portfolio contributed to your competence as a novice teacher?
2. What effect did the portfolio have on your motivation to learn?
3. How did the portfolio influence the role that you played in your own assessment and evaluation of performance?

FIGURE 4.7   Testimonials to the Advantages of Incorporating the Portfolio in Student Teaching

"The portfolio contains a lot of valuable information about the student teacher that assists us as we determine an appropriate placement. For example, if we have a student who has an interest in working with and gaining experience in technology, I can assign him or her to a teacher who works directly with integrating computers into the curriculum. Or, if a student is interested in whole language approaches, I have certain teachers who model that daily. The portfolio also helps me to understand where the student has concentrated his preservice training and how we might assist him in gaining additional experiences. Also, we have a better understanding of how he or she can help our children learn." (Principal of the elementary PDS)

"In the past, the supervision of student teachers was controlled by the university. Now it is being shared by the university supervisor and the supervising teachers with input from the student teacher. The portfolio has become a useful guide in assisting us to establish goals for supervision of the preservice teacher and as a tool to assess and evaluate student performance. The portfolio also helps as we engage in collaborative evaluation with the student teacher. I like the way . . . we now have concrete and visible evidence of the student teacher's performance." (Cooperating teacher at the PDS)

"Using the portfolio personalizes the introduction of our student teacher for my students and for me. It also assists me in organizing the student teacher's experiences around the ten standards and ensures that the student is obtaining a well-rounded experience. Working with student teachers and the professor around the portfolio has inspired me to create my own portfolio." (Cooperating teacher at the PDS)

4. How did the portfolio help you to assume more responsibility for your own learning?
5. How did the portfolio help you experience the relationship between effort and results?

Figure 4.8 shows a representative sample of responses of seniors during the exit interview.

Our goal throughout the student teaching experience and during the exit interview is to provide opportunities for beginning teachers to gain a clearer understanding of their developing skills as teachers. The use of portfolios has assisted our faculty and our

---

FIGURE 4.8 Sample of Responses of Seniors during the Exit Interview

"I am more confident as a student teacher and feel validated about my work after having had the opportunity to showcase my best efforts through the development and use of my portfolio."

"I found it was important to remember to take time to process each activity. What we learned about the use of portfolios must be practiced throughout the semester."

"During the sharing of artifacts, I gathered new ideas and strategies for teaching and had my peers affirm my work. This encouraged me to share reflections about my teaching and I was able to identify what part of the portfolio triggered new ideas for me to consider."

"I learned that the portfolio can assist me in presenting my accomplishments during the interview process as well as [be] a vehicle for documenting my professional accomplishments throughout my teaching tenure."

"After talking with other student teachers and sharing our artifacts and information about our classrooms, I understand now why we need to be equipped with so many different teaching strategies."

"One of the major changes is the self-confidence I have gained after completing this experience. As a result of the intensity of the program and the work at the PDS, I have a clearer understanding of what I am doing as a teacher. Although the portfolio was a lot of work, I am glad that I developed one and learned ways it can be used. It helped me to understand why I did what I did and why it was successful or unsuccessful."

"The portfolio documents the time I spent in the classroom and what I accomplished through self-reflection, instruction, and monitoring my professional growth. I feel confident that I will use my portfolio throughout my career."

"I enjoyed using the portfolio during the student teaching experience. I was able to make better decisions about what worked in certain situations."

"The portfolio helped me to construct my philosophy of teaching and learning based on my teaching practices. I was able to monitor my growth as a constructivist teacher and now I can showcase that to administrators and school board members."

"The portfolio entries helped me to reflect more on my teaching. During conferences and interviews, I was asked to describe to the university supervisor and my cooperating teacher my plans, my methods of teaching and assessment, and ways I work with diversity in the classroom. I had to explain in my own mind why I did what I did. The portfolio helped me to understand my actions and to connect my practices to my philosophy of teaching. The process of working through the portfolio helped me to be clear in my thoughts and to show others examples of my work."

---

school-based partners in making the student teaching experience a process through which preservice teachers make a transition from being a student learning about teaching to becoming a teacher engaged in learning about learning.

CONCLUSION

Providing students with support as they develop their portfolios is important to the premise of portfolio assessment. Mentor/peer support, the PDS, and three conferencing checkpoints enable students to meet objectives and standards. Collaborative, supportive portfolio systems assist students in documenting their learning in appropriate ways, self-reflecting, and setting goals. Such support provides an environment in which they can witness clear applications of the theory that your program espouses. Students need partners as they build their portfolios: faculty, mentors, peers, and partnership schools. Waiting until they are ready to finish the program to assess students' performances will not ensure that they are developing as the teachers you want them to be. Ongoing support and formative assessment are necessary.

Chapter 5 describes how portfolios and performance assessments can strengthen the process of program evaluation.

▶ 5

Assessing Program Quality

Our set of standards, adapted from those developed by the Interstate New Teacher Assessment and Support Consortium (Darling-Hammond, 1992), describes what it is we want our students to know and be able to do when they have completed the program. Portfolios serve as a vehicle for focusing both student and faculty attention on the standards and providing a structure for students to document their competence in the knowledge and skills contained within those standards.

The portfolio serves an additional and equally critical function: It is a tool to assess program effectiveness. Standards are simply empty shells unless we have concrete, visible evidence that our students are meeting them. Portfolios provide us with a window into our students' abilities to achieve and demonstrate the knowledge and skills described in the standards. For teacher preparation programs to be accountable, it will become increasingly important that we be able to show, not simply just tell, the public, political leaders, and accrediting agencies what our students know and what they can do.

Standards and portfolios make a powerful combination, in that "they guide the program's feedback systems—feedback to learners about their strengths and weaknesses, so that they can set goals for growth; feedback to professors, so that they can improve their performance. And finally, feedback to the program or the system itself, again for the purpose of improvement" (Diez, 1997, pp. 6–7). Portfolios built on a comprehensive set of standards give students, professors, and administrators valuable information about individual, course, and program effectiveness.

PROGRAM ACCREDITATION: CHANGING PARADIGMS

The National Commission on Teaching and America's Future, in *What Matters Most: Teaching for America's Future* (1996), calls for the implementation of rigorous standards for teacher education programs. The report suggests that states can best accomplish this in partnership with the National Council for Accreditation of Teacher Education (NCATE), the largest and most influential teacher education accrediting organization. Historically the accreditation of teacher education programs through NCATE has focused on the "ability of faculty and candidates to articulate the knowledge base and philosophy on which the program is built, examinations of the courses and requirements, admissions and exit criteria, qualifications of faculty, and organization of field experiences . . ." (Elliott, 1997, p. 6). However, the emphasis on curriculum and other input measures to assess program and candidate performance is changing.

In 1998, the National Council for Accreditation of Teacher Education announced plans for "NCATE 2000," a new performance-based system of accreditation in teacher education. "Through its New Professional Teacher Standards Development Project, NCATE is reframing the focus of accreditation standards so that a judgment on program quality is based in large measure on candidate performance" (Elliott, 1997, p. 6). Visiting accrediting teams "will focus increasingly on the performance of the institution and its candidates; there will be a better balance among inputs, processes, and outcomes. More emphasis will be placed on the quality of the candidate work, candidate subject matter knowledge, and demonstrated teaching skill" (Wise, 1998, p. 1). The key question, both for those who deliver the program and those who evaluate it, will be "What do candidates know and what can they do when they graduate from initial and advanced teacher preparation programs?" (Wise, 1998).

This is a major shift in how teacher education programs are assessed. The advanced degrees of faculty, student grades, course content, and so forth will no longer be the sole indicators of program effectiveness. The emphasis is now on candidate performance. "In a performance oriented accreditation framework, more emphasis would be placed on the quality of candidate work and on candidate performance. Examining teams would look at demonstrations of candidate content knowledge and the ability to teach that content effectively, as demonstrated in portfolios, journals, assessment results, evaluations by faculty and cooperating teachers . . ." (Elliott, 1997, p. 7).

For those schools and departments of education that do not want or are unable to meet these standards the potential consequences are severe. In a recent report the National Commission on Teaching and America's Future calls for all schools to be accredited. "Schools that are serious about preparing teachers should take the necessary steps to become accredited. Those that are not willing and able to develop a critical mass of intellectual resources for training teachers should turn their attention to doing other things well" (1996, p. 3).

The initial step in moving to a performance-based program is the development of standards. The process we used to accomplish this has been described in detail in Chapter 1. Once program standards have been developed, it becomes necessary to build a framework within which teacher education candidates can demonstrate what they know and what they can do. One vehicle we utilize is the student portfolio, in which artifacts are placed that demonstrate candidate competence in meeting each of our ten standards.

Both the student portfolio and the process students go through in the development of their portfolios can provide us with potentially valuable data about candidate performance and program effectiveness. Described in the following sections are various data collection techniques we recommend for effective and continuous program evaluation.

COLLECTING DATA FOR PROGRAM ASSESSMENT

As described in the preceding chapter, we have instituted a series of checkpoints for our students as they move through their program. It is at these points that program requirements are checked, portfolios are presented to faculty members, and our program philosophy is discussed. We suggest that data be collected at each of these checkpoints to assess program effectiveness. No single piece of information can or should be used for program assessment. In order for the assessment to be reliable and valid, data should come from a variety of sources and be collected at various points in a student's program.

Junior-Level Checkpoint

The Junior-Level checkpoint in our system involves an individual conference between a student and a faculty member. Data for program assessment are not actually generated at the conference itself, but are the result of students completing an Artifacts Checklist prior to the conference. It is placed in the portfolio for the faculty member to review several days before the actual conference. A copy is made of the checklist at the time of the conference.

The checklist (reproduced in Appendix A) contains the names of fifty possible artifacts students could place in their portfolios. Every document contained in the portfolio must be noted in the Artifacts Checklist. Students identify each artifact as a performance assessment task or project, a self-generated document, or a self-selected document. Students also indicate under which standard a particular artifact or document is placed. As students continue to progress through their program, the Artifact Checklist is continually updated. Thus, at any point in time, the checklist provides a snapshot of the contents of a student's portfolio. In addition, we can also determine those standards that are being met with portfolio artifacts and those other standards that have been neglected.

The Artifacts Checklist provides several pieces of important information. The first involves coverage of the ten standards. The goal of our program is to provide students with assignments and experiences related to each of the ten standards. The Artifacts Checklist, therefore, can tell us at any point in time during a student's program whether or not we are succeeding at this goal.

Suppose we see a pattern developing over a period of time in which few if any artifacts appear under Standard #10 dealing with partnerships. This could be interpreted in one of two ways. Perhaps students are being provided with assignments and experiences related to partnerships and simply do not or cannot make the connection between the assignment/experience and the standard. Or perhaps we are failing to provide our students with assignments and experiences that relate to the knowledge, skills, and/or behaviors contained within the standard.

Either scenario has implications for program delivery. If the first scenario is true, we need to do a better job at making the connection between what we are having students do in our classes or field experiences and the relevant standards. The connection may be clear in the instructor's mind, but that is of little value unless the student sees the connection as well.

If the second scenario rings true, we can revisit our courses and their corresponding performance assessment tasks and projects to determine where such an assignment or experience could be provided. It is incumbent upon us to ensure to the best of our ability that our students are provided with assignments and experiences that engage them in addressing all of the ten standards.

A second potentially valuable piece of information from the Artifacts Checklist involves the placement of artifacts. Course instructors often design an assignment or project with particular standards in mind. For instance, a unit of study is an assignment in the elementary social studies methods class. The assignment is designed in such a way as to incorporate the skills and knowledge described in four standards. Suppose students frequently place this unit of study under standards other than the ones intended. Course instructors may have to examine the way the project is described and delivered in class. Perhaps the connection between an assignment and the relevant standards is not being made clear. Students may be completing the assignment without a clear understanding of the skills and knowledge being utilized. We have all had moments in class when students simply complete an assignment in rote fashion, not truly comprehending what they are doing or why they are doing it. The connection between the assessment and the skills and knowledge contained in the relevant standards needs to be understood by students.

The Artifacts Checklist can also tell us whether certain artifacts are being overused. Suppose that, upon examining the summary data from the checklist, we find students using lesson plans to satisfy an inordinate number of standards. This result would warrant a reexamination of the performance assessment tasks and other course assignments. We should be providing our students with a variety of experiences in their courses and fieldwork. If lesson plans are showing up under most or all of the standards, that necessary variety may not be present. This scenario is less likely to occur, however, if a department practices the curriculum mapping strategy described later in this chapter.

Senior-Level Checkpoint

The culminating experience in most teacher education programs is student teaching, an extensive field experience in which students put into practice the knowledge, skills, and attitudes learned in methods courses. In a controlled setting, under the supervision of a cooperating teacher and a university supervisor, students make the transition between preservice and inservice status.

The senior checkpoint, unlike the one conducted during the junior year, is not a single conference between student and instructor. Rather, this checkpoint, as described in Chapter 4, is characterized by a series of interviews, observations, and conferences. The participants include not only the student and university supervisor, but also school practitioners such as classroom teachers and administrators. These multiple sources of feedback provide the student with valuable information about teaching performance and behavior and can also furnish the department with significant data regarding program effectiveness. During the interviews, observations, and conferences described here, data can be collected and used in summary fashion to assess the effectiveness of the student's preparation.

Initial Conference
with a Cooperating Teacher

Students schedule conferences with their cooperating teachers at the beginning of the student teaching experience to present their portfolios. The purpose of the conference is two-fold: First, it is a way for students to introduce themselves to the cooperating teachers, and, second, the cooperating teachers can review the portfolios contents and use that information to set goals and objectives for the students during the student teaching experience.

During the presentation of the portfolio at the initial conference the cooperating teacher looks for areas of strength as reflected by multiple artifacts under a specific standard. Examining standards that have few artifacts identifies gaps in a student's experience. Both strengths and weaknesses are noted and then utilized to establish goals for the student during the student teaching experience. The comments from the cooperating teachers can then be summarized and returned to the department.

Student Teaching Observations

One of the most valuable sources of data for program assessment comes from the forms used by the university supervisor during a series of formal observations over the course of the student teaching experience. When we adopted the ten standards for use in our department, we reexamined the evaluation forms used in student teaching. As the experiences students receive in our classes are centered on the ten standards, we thought it essential to assess students' classroom performance using an instrument that reflected those standards. In other words, the behavioral indicators that make up the forms should mirror the skills, knowledge, and attitudes contained in the standards.

The data collected using the student teaching observation forms can be important for several reasons. First, and perhaps most importantly, these data reflect the actual classroom performance of our students. All the experiences provided for our students up to this point focus on one objective: the development of expert classroom teachers. The observations conducted during student teaching by the university supervisor provide us with concrete and visible evidence that our students are meeting that goal.

In addition to providing us with a glimpse of a student's classroom performance, data from the student teaching observation forms are important for the purpose of program assessment. These forms are produced in triplicate, and copies are given to the student and the cooperating teacher during the post-observation conference. At the conclusion of every semester the summary data from the observation forms, as well as those from the forms described in the next section, can be compiled and reviewed by the department. The data can then be used to identify areas within the program that may need to be revised or strengthened. For instance, if the results from instruments indicate students are having difficulty with some aspect of classroom management, we could review those courses and experiences related to that particular standard and make appropriate changes.

Mid-Point Assessment
and Final Evaluation

At the mid-point of each student teaching assignment and at the conclusion of each assignment, formative and summative evaluative data are collected and presented to the student teacher in a conference with both the university supervisor and cooperating teacher. The purpose of the mid-point assessment is to identify for the student teacher areas of strength and weakness, so that goals for improvement can be established and addressed during the second half of the placement. The final evaluation represents a cumulative assessment of the student's performance in the classroom. The report is completed by the cooperating teacher and reviewed with the student teacher during an exit conference. Again, it is suggested that indicators used to assess student performance at both the mid-point and the conclusion of student teaching reflect the standards adopted by the department. These evaluations are collected and analyzed by the department.

Portfolio Days

As described in Chapter 4, celebratory and assessment activities take place as part of what we call "Portfolio Days." Student teachers return to the college campus for a day to make presentations of their portfolios to sophomores and juniors, to run a workshop on portfolio development, and, every 2 years, to exhibit their portfolios for the university community and local school teachers and administrators. The latter activity is structured in such a way as to provide program assessment data.

Students exhibit their portfolios in a performance center on campus in much the same way that a poster session is organized at a professional conference. Tables are set up around the room and students display their portfolios and the artifacts contained within them for visitors to examine. In addition to other university students, faculty, and administrators, we encourage public school personnel to attend. All those attending the session complete a feedback form. Particular attention is paid to the comments of the public school personnel.

Surveys

For comprehensive and effective program assessment to occur, evaluative data need to be collected at various points in the program and from multiple sources. As described in the preceding sections, data are collected during the junior- and senior-level checkpoints, involving self-reports from students, conferences with faculty, observations of college supervisors, and many others. As a final source of program assessment data, we survey our recent graduates and the elementary and middle school teachers who have worked with our student teachers during the preceding academic year. The Survey of Recent Graduates (see Figure 5.1) and The Survey of Cooperating Teachers (see Figure 5.2) are mailed to the targeted population every spring. A self-addressed, postage-paid envelope is included to encourage a high response rate.

FIGURE 5.1   **The Survey of Recent Graduates**

The Elementary/Early Childhood Education department is continually assessing the quality of the experiences you have received here at California University of Pennsylvania. Please take a few moments to complete this survey. The results will be anonymous and reported only in summary form. Thank you for your time and patience.

1. Major (check one):

    _____ Early Childhood Education   _____ Early Childhood/Elementary Education

    _____ Elementary Education   _____ Elementary/Middle School Education

    _____ Elementary/Special Education   _____ Early Childhood/Special Education

2. Are you a transfer student? _____ Yes (# of CUP credits _____) _____ No

3. Gender: _____ Female   _____ Male

4. Age: _____ 21–25 years   _____ 26–30 years   _____ over 30 years

Please read each statement and circle the number that best describes your feeling about that statement.

	Strongly Agree	Agree	Disagree	Strongly Disagree
5. I am knowledgeable in the content matter found at the Elementary/Early Childhood grades.	4	3	2	1
6. I am able to teach the content matter found at the Elementary/Early Childhood grades.	4	3	2	1
7. I understand the central concepts of the disciplines taught at the Elementary/Early Childhood grades.	4	3	2	1
8. I understand how children learn and develop.	4	3	2	1
9. I understand how students differ in their approaches to learning.	4	3	2	1
10. I am familiar with a variety of instructional strategies.	4	3	2	1

FIGURE 5.1   *Continued*

	Strongly Agree	Agree	Disagree	Strongly Disagree
11. My instruction is based upon a philosophy of teaching.	4	3	2	1
12. I am able to effectively plan for instruction.	4	3	2	1
13. I actively seek out opportunities to grow professionally.	4	3	2	1
14. I make an effort to foster relationships with school colleagues.	4	3	2	1
15. I effectively teach the content matter found at the Elementary/Early Childhood grades.	4	3	2	1
16. I provide learning opportunities that support students' cognitive development.	4	3	2	1
17. I provide learning opportunities that support students' affective development.	4	3	2	1
18. I provide learning opportunities that support students' psychomotor development.	4	3	2	1
19. I create instructional opportunities that are adapted to diverse learners.	4	3	2	1
20. I use a variety of instructional strategies in my teaching.	4	3	2	1
21. I am able to promote students' critical-thinking and problem-solving skills in my teaching.	4	3	2	1
22. I am able to motivate my students.	4	3	2	1
23. I am able to create a positive learning environment.	4	3	2	1
24. I actively engage my students in learning.	4	3	2	1
25. I use effective verbal communication skills in the classroom to enhance learning.	4	3	2	1
26. I use effective nonverbal communication skills in the classroom to enhance learning.	4	3	2	1

Continued

FIGURE 5.1   *Continued*

	Strongly Agree	Agree	Disagree	Strongly Disagree
27. I use different media in the classroom.	4	3	2	1
28. I use formal assessment strategies to evaluate student learning.	4	3	2	1
29. I use informal assessment strategies to evaluate student learning.	4	3	2	1
30. I evaluate my teaching.	4	3	2	1

31. How has the development of your portfolio been of value to you?

FIGURE 5.2   The Survey of Cooperating Teachers

The Elementary/Early Childhood Education department is continually assessing the quality of the experiences we provide our students at California University of Pennsylvania. In light of significant changes in our program during the last three years, we are attempting to gather data regarding the performance and preparation of our student teachers. Please take a few moments to complete this survey. The results will be anonymous and reported only in summary form. Thank you for your time and patience.

1. Grade level(s) currently taught: _____

2. Years of teaching experience: _____

3. Gender: _____ Female _____ Male

4. How many California University of Pennsylvania student teachers have you worked with during the past three years? _____

Please consider only those student teachers you have worked with during the last three years when responding to the following items. Circle the number that best describes your feeling about that statement.

	Strongly Agree	Agree	Disagree	Strongly Disagree
California University of Pennsylvania student teachers . . .				
5. are knowledgeable in the content matter found at the Elementary/Early Childhood grades.	4	3	2	1
6. are able to teach the content matter found at the Elementary/Early Childhood grades.	4	3	2	1
7. understand the central concepts of the disciplines taught at the Elementary/Early Childhood grades.	4	3	2	1
8. understand how children learn and develop.	4	3	2	1
9. understand how students differ in their approaches to learning.	4	3	2	1
10. are familiar with a variety of instructional strategies.	4	3	2	1

Continued

FIGURE 5.2 *Continued*

	Strongly Agree	Agree	Disagree	Strongly Disagree
11. base instruction upon a philosophy of teaching.	4	3	2	1
12. effectively plan for instruction.	4	3	2	1
13. actively seek out opportunities to grow professionally.	4	3	2	1
14. make an effort to foster relationships with school colleagues.	4	3	2	1
15. effectively teach the content matter found at the Elementary/Early Childhood grades.	4	3	2	1
16. provide learning opportunities that support students' cognitive development.	4	3	2	1
17. provide learning opportunities that support students' affective development.	4	3	2	1
18. provide learning opportunities that support students' psychomotor development.	4	3	2	1
19. create instructional opportunities that are adapted to diverse learners.	4	3	2	1
20. use a variety of instructional strategies in their teaching.	4	3	2	1
21. promote students' critical-thinking and problem-solving skills in their teaching.	4	3	2	1
22. are able to motivate students.	4	3	2	1
23. are able to create a positive learning environment.	4	3	2	1
24. actively engage students in learning.	4	3	2	1
25. use effective verbal communication skills in the classroom to enhance learning.	4	3	2	1
26. use effective nonverbal communication skills in the classroom to enhance learning.	4	3	2	1
27. use different media in the classroom.	4	3	2	1

FIGURE 5.2 *Continued*

	Strongly Agree	Agree	Disagree	Strongly Disagree
28. use formal assessment strategies to evaluate student learning.	4	3	2	1
29. use informal assessment strategies to evaluate student learning.	4	3	2	1
30. evaluate their own teaching.	4	3	2	1

31. The Elementary/Early Childhood Education Department requires all majors to develop portfolios. Could you comment on this requirement?

Each survey begins with a few items to collect demographic data about the respondent. The surveys each consist of thirty items presented in a four-point Likert scale format, ranging from "Strongly Agree" to "Strongly Disagree" or "Always" to "Never." Like the other instruments and surveys discussed previously, the items correspond to the ten department standards. Each of the ten standards corresponds to one to three survey items. This makes it possible to not only obtain an overall picture of our students' competence, but also to isolate one or more standards for review.

Although we collect data from both students and cooperating teachers during student teaching, the timing and structure of these surveys yield different and potentially valuable results. The surveys come at the very end of the students' teacher preparation program, thus providing an opportunity for them to reflect back on the totality of their experiences. Students complete the survey on their own time, without a faculty member, college supervisor, or cooperating teacher observing the process. Our assumption is that survey responses may thus be a little more honest and reflective of the students' true attitudes about the program.

The same assumption holds true for the cooperating teacher survey. When cooperating teachers provide assessment data related to their student teachers' performance, the students themselves and the college supervisor are often present or, at the very least, have access to the results. Data collected under such circumstances could obviously reflect less of an accurate or honest appraisal and more of what the cooperating teacher believes either the student or college supervisor wants to hear. An anonymous survey will more likely produce valid and reliable results.

Data from the Survey of Recent Graduates reflect perceptions held by students about their skills, knowledge, and attitudes toward teaching in relation to our ten standards. In most cases, scores on a self-report survey such as this may be slightly misleading, as most people tend to possess an inflated view of their own abilities. Thus, we balance the data we get from our recent graduates with data from practitioners, those teachers who have recently worked with our student teachers. Results of a correlational study show that there is a strong positive relationship between the perceptions of students about their own abilities and the perceptions held by cooperating teachers about the abilities of the student teachers.

Performance Assessment
Curriculum Mapping

One final activity we recommend is a variation of curriculum mapping. Although it involves faculty and not students, the results provide an overall picture of the experiences and assignments we require of our students. This information should be seen as simply one additional piece of the program assessment puzzle.

Using the Artifact Checklist, faculty members plot all products and documents that are a part of their performance assessment tasks and projects. This provides us with an overall summary of the standards being addressed through the use of the performance assessments in all our courses. A faculty member then writes a short description of his or her performance assessment task (see Figure 5.3). As you can see from the example in Figure 5.3, specific parts of the document or artifact are identified and then connected to standards through behavioral indicators.

Every instructor produces these documents for each course taught, and performance assessment descriptions are collected in a large notebook. Following each description is an outstanding example of the corresponding performance assessment produced by one of our students. What we then have in a single notebook are all the performance assessments, behavioral indicators connecting each task or project to specific program standards, and an example of each task or project produced by a student. This notebook is made available to faculty for study and analysis. It allows us to determine whether certain types of artifacts are being overused (e.g., lesson plans), and it permits us to ascertain whether there is an overemphasis on some standards while others are minimally addressed. The notebook is also an effective exhibit, showing students, faculty, administrators, and accrediting agencies the assignments and experiences that constitute our program. An example from the summary section of that notebook is contained in Figure 5.4.

FIGURE 5.3 Performance Assessment Project for Field Experience with Infants, Toddlers, and Preschoolers

Description

Students enrolled in this course practice and demonstrate communication skills that are likely to facilitate optimal language development in young children. They practice speaking to infants and toddlers using a variety of indirect language stimulation techniques. Students document their progress using these techniques through video taping, observation reports, and transcripts of conversations. They practice direct language stimulation in the form of open-ended questions when working with preschoolers. This skill is documented in a lesson plan and lesson transcript. The students analyze the effects of these strategies on the children participating.

Standards Addressed

Standard #2, Knowledge of Human Development and Learning

Behavioral Indicators:

1. The students observe and record examples of young children's language.
2. The students compare the language output of selected infants and toddlers before receiving indirect language stimulation and after.
3. The students analyze the language patterns of preschool children when open-ended questions are used.

Standard #6, Communication Skills

Behavioral Indicators:

1. The students use parallel talk with infants and toddlers.
2. The students use descriptive talk with infants and toddlers.
3. The students use self-talk with infants and toddlers.
4. The students use expansion techniques with infants, toddlers, and preschoolers.
5. The students develop and use effective questions with preschoolers.

Performances

Speaking to a young child around 1 year of age using indirect language.
Teaching a lesson to preschoolers using direct language.

Products

Video or audio tapes
Observation report with partial conversation transcripts.
Lesson plan with partial conversation transcripts.

Portfolio Requirement

One document including the observation report and lesson plan is required.

FIGURE 5.4   **An Example of a Performance Assessment Summary**

Course	Performance Assessment	Standards Addressed
EDE 211—Instructional Strategies	Personal Philosophy of Education	7
ECE 203—Field: Infant, Toddler, Preschool	Facilitating Language Development	2, 6
ECE 304—Thematic Teaching in Early Childhood	Building an Integrated Curriculum	1, 4, 7, 8

CONCLUSION

Adopting a set of standards and then redesigning our curriculum to focus on the knowledge, skills, and attitudes contained in those standards has been a long and challenging process. The maintenance of this system depends on the timely and systematic collection of program assessment data. Having a set of standards and a means by which students document their competence in regards to those standards is pointless unless data are collected that provide reliable and valid evidence that the standards are being met. The portfolios themselves and the process through which students develop their portfolios provide an excellent means and structure for collecting program assessment data.

The final chapter will describe how the assessment system presented in this text unites to form the total foundation upon which our work rests. In this chapter we share the way this system appears today and what we have learned about ourselves as a result of implementing a major change in our department.

▶ 6

Learning As We Go: Continuing the Work of Program Self-Evaluation

Perhaps the hardest part of any endeavor that brings about change is the first part—getting started. In the previous five chapters of this book we have explained how faculty members in our program implemented a portfolio system of assessments that reflect our program philosophy and standards. We have shown how each part of the system works and have offered suggestions on how these parts might work for your teacher education program as you get started in this endeavor. In this chapter we shall review how these parts link together to form the whole foundation upon which our work rests. In addition, we shall explain how this system looks to us today and what we have learned about ourselves as a result of implementing a major change in our program. Reviewing the system that we have presented here, and examining some of the hurdles that we have attempted to overcome, can help you move toward that first step.

THE WHOLE PICTURE

Our portfolio assessment system began with a vision. In 1992 our department chairperson asked us to form a committee that had only one task: Dream about the future. Quite literally, that was just about all the direction we had (purposefully so). While it was refreshing to be on a committee that had no rules, no intended outcome, and no report to write, it was also intimidating. We were asked to imagine what our department could be like in 5 years and to decide what it would take to head our program in that direction.

With that one visionary, swift "kick in the pants," we were off and running toward the future. This book summarizes what was done. Our program is now vastly different from what it was a few years ago. There are many things still left to be done; there always will be. But we feel sure that our students are now able to show others what good teaching is all about, and that our program prepares them to do this.

All the pieces that go together to form our portfolio assessment system are shown in Figure 6.1. In this graphic organizer you can see that the philosophy of our program, constructivism, is the starting point for all else. This leads to all the components of the system, ending with assessment at three checkpoints. The account that follows explains how the pieces make up the whole picture. In so doing, we shall review for you the work that we have done.

As explained in Chapter 1, constructivism is the philosophy that our faculty members agree upon as the underlying basis for all our work. There are varying emphases of definition of this philosophy for all of us, but, as one faculty member put it, "In general, no matter what we do or what we say, we all agree that children learn best by being involved." Our model is at the top of the graphic organizer.

From our model, standards that we hold ourselves and our students responsible for were written. The ten standards that we use were adapted from INTASC, but they are also our own, in that we decided which parts of the INTASC standards needed to be changed to fit our own beliefs about teaching and learning. Many changes were suggested by faculty members themselves. We also received

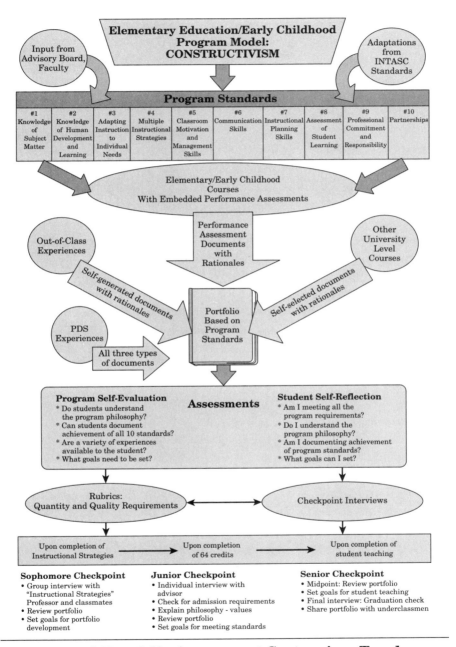

FIGURE 6.1   A Portfolio Assessment System in a Teacher Education Program

input from our advisory board, a group of teachers, administrators, students, and graduates who met with us on a semester basis. Specific changes have been made as a result of these advisory board meetings, from rewording of the standards to creating new courses. The standards are listed across the top of the graphic organizer in Figure 6.1, under the model.

The picture of the portfolio in the middle of Figure 6.1 represents our students' portfolios, which contain documents that reflect their ability to perform all ten of our standards. Also shown are the sources of their documents. These artifacts are of three types: (1) required performance assessment projects or tasks from each of our courses, (2) documents that the students select from other classes at the university level, and (3) documents that the students generate based on their work outside of class. Any of these three types of documents might reflect work done in our Professional Development School, which provides a rich context for work in a school setting that mirrors our philosophy. All documents that are inserted in the portfolio must include rationales that summarize the experience, explain their relationship to the standards they represent, and clarify their role in the professional growth of the student.

Assessment, as shown on the bottom portion of Figure 6.1, is a multifaceted endeavor. We use this portfolio system to evaluate ourselves and our work in the program, as well as the performances of our students. Everyone involved—faculty as well as the student body—uses the rubrics and the checkpoint interviews to determine how well the philosophy and the standards are understood, how well students are able to perform our standards, and what short-term and long-range goals need to be set. Specific tasks are accomplished at each checkpoint, as shown on the time line at the bottom of the figure.

In summary, the portfolio assessment system that is shown in Figure 6.1 is the plan that we follow to make sure that we can answer the questions "What do we think good teachers ought to be able to know and do?" and "Can teachers who are graduates of our program demonstrate that they know and do these things?"

TACKLING THE TOUGH CHALLENGES

We assume you are reading this book because you are interested in assessing the value of portfolios, starting a portfolio assessment system, or enhancing one that you already have in place. There are compelling reasons for doing so, as we have already discussed. There are also challenges to this work, which can encourage you to solve problems or can impede your progress. The section that follows discusses some of the challenges that we encountered and ways that we attempted to meet them—and are continuing to do so.

Overcoming Resistance to Change

Any change in the way business is done on a daily basis is difficult. This was certainly true of our work in this program. While many of us embraced this portfolio system as an exciting way to meet standards, others of us questioned its value for arriving at our goals. There are four ways that we have grappled with these differences: focusing on what unites us, replacing rather than adding on, holding faculty retreats, and involving all faculty members.

Focusing on What Unites Us
All of us, even though we have a great variety of differences in teaching style and viewpoints on ways children learn, seem to agree that children must be actively engaged in their learning, which is the broadest conceptualization of constructivism. Therefore, this is always the returning point when we disagree or have problems with technical details. Making sure that what we implement in our program leads back to the understanding of constructivism is often a solidifying measure.

Replacing Rather Than Adding On
Innovation and paradigm shifts can become burdensome, even overwhelming, when they bring with them numerous activities that must be added to an already full schedule. "One critical factor in overcoming resistance to change is an awareness that what is being proposed is not an add-on, but a rethinking of the way we work"

(Diez, 1998, p. 143). While it is impossible to avoid some new demands on schedules, it is often possible to replace some old structures or integrate the new demands with the old structures. This is what we tried to do in order to gain the cooperation of all those involved in the portfolio and performance assessment model being developed for our program. There are several examples of letting this type of thinking guide us. First, we chose to introduce our vision of teaching and our portfolio requirements in an already existing course, rather than establishing a new workshop or seminar. As a second example, we already had in place junior qualifications for admission to teacher education. Rather than adding another interview at the junior year for portfolio review, we redesigned the existing interview.

Finally, many existing practices in the student teaching experience were adjusted to accommodate a more deliberate emphasis on the adopted standards and portfolio assessment. Introductory meetings with cooperating teachers had long been in place; now they include a portfolio review. Existing observation forms were revised to more clearly reflect the standards. When portfolio updating was found to be a difficult "add-on" to the already heavy demands of student teaching, a few days between assignments were freed for valuable reflecting, goal setting, and portfolio documentation. Your faculty members and students will appreciate all attempts to minimize additional activities and demands as you establish innovative assessment procedures by replacing or adjusting existing structures.

Holding Faculty Retreats

Getting the faculty away from the office for 2 days, in a relaxing mountain setting, allows us to tackle some of our thornier issues in a nonthreatening way. We hold these retreats at the beginning of every school year, and our earliest retreats were essential for building the portfolio system as it exists today. Because the system is in place, we can now devote our retreat agenda to other items. However, we have learned the value of team-building exercises and have continued to incorporate them, regardless of the agenda of the retreat. We have also learned that listening to the voices of experience is important; thus, we invite retired and *emeriti* faculty to attend these retreats and participate in curriculum building and planning. Student representatives and faculty representatives from our Professional Development School have attended as well, which gives us additional perspectives from which to view our work. Exercises such as the one depicted in Figure 6.2 have helped us value each other as individuals who have one goal in mind: educating our future teachers.

Involving All Faculty Members
While the need to involve all faculty members seems to be an obvious point, we found that its importance could easily escape us. With numerous faculty members who have very busy schedules and a multitude of responsibilities, it was sometimes difficult to make sure that everyone had some voice in our portfolio system. Indeed, we became painfully aware on occasions that this was not always happening. Thus, we agreed that a departmental curriculum committee would always be needed in our program, and its focus would be on continuing to update our philosophical statement, our standards, and our assessment system. Task force committees are to be formed from this committee to tackle specific issues such as the rewriting of documents or revising of rubrics. These task force committees include all members of the department—full-time and part-time—not just the members of the curriculum committee.

We also agreed that we would honor and value each other's work. Embedding performance assessments into all of our courses was a major step in the implementation of the portfolio system. Some faculty created performance assessment projects that took over large parts of their courses. Others were more comfortable with more discrete tasks. Flexibility in the way we developed performance assessments was important, and involvement by all was absolutely necessary. We are still struggling with finding meaningful real-life tasks that are feasible for doing in the time allotted for both faculty and students, but we have found that ongoing conversations and sharing of ideas with each other about our work ease the difficulty.

FIGURE 6.2   **Exercise for Accomplishing a Goal at a Faculty Retreat**

Retreat Team Activity:
Writing Behavioral Indicators of the Ten Standards for Teachers

Our students document their achievements and developing competencies around the ten standards adopted by their department. A logical next step is that the evaluations they receive in student teaching also focus on these standards. In order for cooperating teachers to focus their evaluation of student teaching on standards, it is necessary that we as a faculty, representative cooperating teachers, and representative students agree on observable behaviors that would indicate performance criteria for the ten standards.

We shall be using a brainstorming strategy for writing behavioral indicators. Because this is a brainstorming activity, it is important not to evaluate any of the suggestions at first, to encourage creativity and the free flow of ideas. Here is how it will work. Everyone at a table will be working on the same standard. As you think about the standard, ask yourselves, "What in actual behavior would a student teacher do that would indicate that he or she had achieved competence or appropriate performance of this standard?" When you have an idea, write it on a slip of paper. Then read it aloud to those at your table. This may give other group members related ideas. However, no one should evaluate the suggestion at any way at this point. Soon another group member reads a statement and adds it to the pile of potential indicators.

Only after time has been called will each group review the indicators, combining some, eliminating some, and perhaps revising some. A list of five to ten good choices should be put on chart paper to share with the total group. The slips of paper with all approved indicators should be given to our secretary for typing a pool of indicators appropriate for various evaluation forms. Paperclip these together with a label all the "good indicators" for each standard worked on.

To keep uniformity, please write all indicators so they begin with an observable verb, with the subject of the sentence assumed to be the "The student teacher . . ." Here are some examples:

Establishes age-appropriate rules for classroom behavior (Standard #5).

Makes use of open-ended questions to solicit students' ideas (Standard #5).

Keeping an Eye on the Big Picture

It was not until after we had begun implementation of portfolios that we became aware that the details of managing the program could overshadow the reason we began portfolio development in the first place: to send good teachers into our schools. For a while it seemed as if we were becoming successful at putting the wheels in motion, yet we were not sure of where this machine was going! One example of this is in our program evaluation. We knew that it is necessary to make sure that all our students are able to perform all of the ten standards we have adopted. However, when designing performance assessments at the onset of our program, we did not grasp the importance of this. We were anxious to design high-quality assessment projects or tasks for each individual course, but we did not attend to the balance of standards that our program as a whole would address. We were not sure that all ten standards were evenly distributed across our courses. Thus, we have begun the process of curriculum mapping, described in Chapter 5. This will help us determine holes in our program and lead us to brainstorming ways to close these gaps.

Relying on the Advisory Board

When we first began, the Advisory Board had a prominent place in the building of our portfolio system. As we became more involved with our work and the trial-and-error process of implementation, we did not call upon this board as often, especially after our PDS partnership was formed. However, the board is made up of many people in our community, outside our PDS. They can offer excellent insights into the needs of new teachers as they enter the workforce, giving us many suggestions for creating change. In addition, this is a useful meeting ground for us to voice our concerns, such as the fact that some administrators in local school districts do not look at portfolios when they interview prospective new teachers. Thus, we see the Advisory Board as an important part of our future plans for curriculum development.

THE PICTURE OF OUR FUTURE

As we said, this work is not complete. The dreaming is not yet finished. There are many facets of the portfolio system that we still need to develop and some parts that may need to be refined as we move forward. The remainder of this chapter discusses some specific goals that we feel need to continue to be addressed in our program development. We present them here so that you may anticipate areas that you may address in your own program.

Preparing Students for Interviews

Upon completion of our program, all of our students have built a portfolio that documents their abilities to perform ten teaching standards. In the past many of our students have done an excellent job of transforming their presentation portfolio that has guided them throughout their academic tenure in our program into a presentation portfolio that will showcase their abilities needed for a particular job. Recent graduates of our program have worried about their use of the portfolio in an interview, because they have heard about or witnessed administrators who pay little or no attention to their portfolio.

Some of our faculty members incorporate strategies for using the portfolio as a marketing tool in their student teaching seminars; however, time does not permit them to develop this fully. School administrators and inservice teachers from our PDS, as well as some of our recent graduates, have been called upon to visit seminars and talk with students about what takes place during interviews and how to present their portfolios so that interviewers value them more. One of our goals is to develop this further into a workshop presentation and implement it more systematically. We would also like to share our work with local administrators who are not involved in our PDS, so that the value of portfolios can become more appreciated in other places.

Using the Portfolio beyond Graduation

Our work at the PDS has shown us that most of the teachers there value the use of portfolios in their own classrooms. In addition, some of them use portfolios in their own professional development and instructional programs. Teachers share with our students how they use portfolios and standards for national certification, tenure, work around certain themes, and applications for grants and funding. In fact, a few teachers and a university faculty member created a "Partnership Portfolio," which showcases the work we do in our joint endeavors. It is important to us that our students understand how portfolios can be a regular part of their professional lives after they graduate and obtain teaching positions. Thus, we have set goals to do more modeling in our own classes, using our own professional portfolios as teaching tools. We have also begun to explore the range of possible uses of portfolios, perhaps in fields other than our own, to incorporate in our courses.

Graduate Programs

The portfolio system described in this book was largely designed for our undergraduate teacher preparation program. In response to accreditation standards for our graduate programs, as well as a reflection of our beliefs about the strength of this system, we are beginning to require portfolio work of our graduate students as well. These programs have unique features that make the same portfolio system inapplicable to them; therefore, the way we use portfolios may be a bit different. However, our experience with the undergraduate program has prepared us for problems and hurdles we may encounter along the way.

Accountability

One of the thornier issues that we have grappled with is the problem of what to do with students who do not perform standards satisfactorily. Because our portfolio system is an enabling model, we use our checkpoints to help students set goals, build on their strengths to improve their weaknesses, and work together to solve problems that they may have related to the standards. We also depend on each other to make sure that performance assessments are required in each of our courses and that we hold our students to criteria for excellence when evaluating students in our courses. Thus, theoretically, we would have no unsatisfactory documents in any portfolio that reaches the senior-level checkpoint.

However, with a large student population and faculty, even the most well-designed system is subject to flaws. In addition, our rubrics, which delineate our criteria for quality, depend upon faculty judgment in some categories. Thus, we do still have students who complete portfolios that might be considered unsatisfactory to some of us. This poses a real dilemma around the time of graduation!

We have initiated at least two undertakings in order to alleviate some of these problems. First, we use our department curriculum committee to orchestrate continuous improvement through activities such as refining and revising our rubrics and our checkpoint interview procedures. New forms, checklists, and policies sometimes become necessary. Second, we have begun to explore the possibility of offering orientation sessions each year to all new faculty members, including temporary ones. This is especially important because of our dependence on course-embedded performance assessments. Any faculty member who does not use these assessments, for whatever reason, does our students a disservice. Therefore, we want to make sure that all new faculty fully understand our program and its portfolio system.

CONCLUSION

The journey to where we are now—a teacher preparation program that values performance based on standards—has been a challenging and yet satisfying one. As one faculty member remarked early on in our work, "This is the most professionally rewarding committee I've ever served on." That is something not often said of university committee work!

Such challenges and rewards await you as you work to create or enhance your own portfolio and performance assessment system. We offer our model as one that has worked well for us; however, in order to truly shift paradigms, you will need to do more than simply adopt ours. Reexamining the work that you do on a daily basis as well as the needs of your students will help you determine how you can develop an assessment plan that will suit your own teacher preparation program. We feel sure that such a shift in paradigms will eventually meet the ultimate goal of all teacher education programs—to better prepare our future teachers for the work that they face in their classrooms. Making sure that they can do this work is our job well done.

APPENDIX A

Artifacts Checklist

Portfolio Artifacts	St. #1	St. #2	St. #3	St. #4	St. #5	St. #6	St. #7	St. #8	St. #9	St. #10
Anecdotal Records										
Article Summaries or Critiques										
Assessments										
Awards and Certificates										
Bulletin Board Ideas										
Case Studies										
Classroom Management Philosophy										
Community Resources Documents										
Computer Programs										
Cooperative Learning Strategies										
Curriculum Plans										
Essays										
Evaluations										
Field Trip Plans										
Floor Plan										
Goal Statements										
Individualized Plans										

Portfolio Artifacts	St. #1	St. #2	St. #3	St. #4	St. #5	St. #6	St. #7	St. #8	St. #9	St. #10
Interviews with Students, Teachers, Parents										
Journals										
Lesson Plans										
Letters to Parents										
Management and Organization Strategies										
Media Competency										
Meetings and Workshops Log										
Observation Reports										
Peer Critiques										
Philosophy Statement										
Pictures and Photographs										
Portfolio (Student)										
Position Papers										
Problem-Solving Logs										
Professional Development Plans										
Professional Organizations and Committees List										
Professional Readings List										
Projects										
References										
Research Papers										
Rules and Procedures Descriptions										
Schedules										
Seating Arrangement Diagrams										
Self-Assessment Instruments										

Portfolio Artifacts	St. #1	St. #2	St. #3	St. #4	St. #5	St. #6	St. #7	St. #8	St. #9	St. #10
Simulated Experiences										
Student Contracts										
Subscriptions										
Teacher-Made Materials										
Theme Studies										
Transcripts										
Unit Plans										
Video Scenario Critiques										
Volunteer Experience Descriptions										
Work Experience Descriptions										

▶

APPENDIX B

Artifacts Possibilities

The types of documents listed on the next few pages are possible artifacts for students' portfolios and are adapted from *How to Develop a Professional Portfolio: A Manual for Teachers* (Campbell et al., 1997). The definitions were written for students, and each contains two features: a definition of the document as it relates to classes and other learning opportunities, and an explanation of the types of teaching skills that this document may reflect.

Types of Artifacts

Anecdotal Records
These are notes that you have taken in classroom observations or during your own teaching. They may pertain to any of the following: the intellectual, social/emotional, or physical development of a child or some children; personal observations about instructional decisions that you have made; or personal observations of teachers at work. The notes reflect your assessment or child observation skills, your ability to make instructional plans, or your knowledge of child development.

Article Summaries or Critiques
You may have written a summary or evaluation of an article from a professional journal as a class assignment. When including these in your portfolio, choose critiques that address the desired topic very specifically. The title of the article should be reflective of a

chosen standard, making a very obvious connection. This document is especially helpful if your professor has made positive remarks about your work and these remarks are about the standard you wish to document.

The article summary or critique may show your ability to analyze any number of teaching skills. For example, suppose you critiqued an article titled "Getting Parents Involved in Their Children's Education." If you discussed your own ideas about parent involvement in your critique, this document may be able to reflect your knowledge of school–home–community cooperation.

Assessments

Any forms of assessment you have used or developed to measure child performance would be included in this type of document. Examples of assessments are performance tasks, portfolios, teacher-written tests, informal observations or notes, evaluations from lesson plans, formative assessment notes or charts, or summative charts of student developmental levels. You may want to include the actual assessment instrument that you have written, with the children's work on it, if applicable (only one copy is necessary). In addition, you may include notes in a personal journal from observations made during the administration of a standardized test. Your ability to assess children's performance, diagnose progress, and use tests wisely are reflected in this document. In addition, your understanding of child development may be evident.

Awards and Certificates

Copies of letters, awards, or certificates that verify your outstanding contribution to the field of education fit in this category. These could include honors conferred, memberships in honorary professional organizations, community recognition, and volunteer recognition. Your professional commitment is reflected in these types of documents.

Bulletin Board Ideas

After creating a bulletin board, make a copy of your design, or take a photograph of the board. Make sure all spelling, punctuation, and grammar are standard English. This document can be used to show your ability to think creatively, use materials in interesting ways, or motivate students.

Case Studies

A case study is a thorough examination of a student's growth over a period of time. When using this as a document, make sure the student is anonymous. Generally case studies are quite long; therefore, you may want to include a specific part of the paper for documentation of a standard. Your knowledge of child development, as well as your observation skills, may be evident in this document.

Classroom Management Philosophy

This is a written summary of your philosophy of classroom management. Make sure to cite the research and theories that have guided you in the way you influence student behavior and encourage development of self-control. Classroom management skills are evident in this document, as is knowledge of human development.

Community Resources Documents

These might include copies of actual correspondence or a description of less formal contact between you and a community resource. Have you solicited a community resource to provide information in completing a course assignment or to teach a lesson in the classroom? Did you invite a guest speaker into your classroom during a field class or student teaching? These types of correspondence show that you are able to foster positive relationships between the community and the school.

Computer Programs

This includes examples of various programs you have utilized, developed, or have incorporated in your teaching that provide evidence of your ability to use materials in a challenging and appropriate way to encourage active learning.

Also appropriate are programs that demonstrate your ability to conduct on-line searches and research. Examples include ERIC, Education Index, and Internet programs that link teachers worldwide. You can document your abilities by providing the hard copies of these searches, along with an explanation of the reason for your computer searches. These documents reflect your willingness to seek further professional growth.

Cooperative Learning Strategies

Have you planned or taught a lesson using a cooperative learning technique? Cooperative learning is a method of teaching in which students work collaboratively in small groups to solve a problem. This type of group work must be obvious in your lesson. You may want to include a copy of the lesson plan and, if the lesson was actually taught, a statement assessing the effectiveness of the cooperative learning technique. This will document your ability to use cooperative learning as a strategy as well as your ability to manage and motivate a class of students.

Curriculum Plans

These documents are written plans and/or programs designed to organize curriculum. Your curriculum plans can reflect all experiences you have developed for the child while engaged in the process of schooling. Examples may include lesson plans, units, thematic units, learning centers, extracurricular programs, or school-community ventures. These documents portray your instructional planning skills or your ability to use many and varied instructional strategies.

Essays

You can use papers from education courses, English composition, or any other class in which you were required to write an essay. Examine the topic you addressed in your paper to be sure its main idea reflects one of the standards you are using.

This type of artifact could document almost any standard. The question that you wish to answer or the topic you wish to address should be clearly stated at the beginning of the essay. You may want to highlight this, showing its obvious connection to the standard you wish to document. For example, suppose you wrote an essay in a composition class that is titled "Why Suzy Can't Do Math: The Influence of Societal Expectations." Because this is an essay on the differences that gender may make in the perception of students in the home, in the neighborhood, and in school, your understanding of social influences on the education of females becomes evident. This would be a good artifact to document your understanding of the multiple contexts affecting educational decisions.

Evaluations

Any on-the-job performance assessment is an especially important type of evaluation to include in a portfolio. Student teaching is one place where this will occur. You might include actual observations done when you taught a lesson, feedback on a written assignment, or some kind of summative assessment (interim or final evaluation). Make sure there is a relationship between the evaluation comments and the standard.

Field Trip Plans

As a preservice teacher you may have gone on field trips that would be related to one of the standards you have chosen to use. Trips such as these may include visits to teacher centers, libraries, museums, innovative classrooms, other universities, youth centers, rehabilitation centers, or church-related activities. You may document this by including copies of programs, personal journals, agendas, letters of invitation, or memos. Your own notes or observational reports are also helpful. This type of document may provide evidence for a variety of standards. Your professional commitment and responsibility are reflected because of your willingness to seek information outside the college classroom.

You may have attended field trips with a student group. This experience may relate to one of the standards, depending on the nature of the trip and your reaction to it. A well-written reaction paper or journal entry would help document such a trip. For example, suppose you were invited to join your field class on a trip to the children's theater. Your cooperating teacher did a nice job of incorporating this trip into her classroom lessons by reading a book about the play to the children, then having them act it out themselves and write an experience story about the trip. If you write an observational report about this, making notes about the interrelatedness of the activities and the importance of the subject matter to the growth of the students, you can document your knowledge of content and of child development.

If you actually planned a field trip for one of your classes, be sure to document this. Record your lesson plans, your correspondence with the community agents involved, your letter to parents, and any other communication you used. This is strong evidence of your planning skills, knowledge of content, knowledge of human development, and school–home–community cooperation.

Floor Plan
A floor plan is a sketch of the arrangement of space, equipment, and materials you designed in order to meet the needs of a group of students under your supervision. Your ability to use environments and materials appropriately is most closely related to this document. If you include a statement of how this floor plan enhances your classroom management plan, then it also could document your classroom management skills.

Goal Statements
Professional goals are based upon your needs, interests, philosophy of education, and your perception of your role as a teacher. Goal statements assist you in determining where you want to be and provide you with information about how to get there.

Think about the important results you should accomplish in your role as a teacher and record these as goal statements. Remember that any short-term goals you establish should be tied to the longer-term goals you have identified in conjunction with your philosophy of education. Periodically review and evaluate your accomplishments in relation to your goal statements. You may wish to list your accomplishments associated with each goal. You will establish new goals as you refine your philosophy of education, your role as a teacher, and your expectations. It is important to keep your list of goal statements current. These statements might appear at the beginning of your portfolio or as documentation of your professional commitment.

Individualized Plans
Children with special needs sometimes need tasks to be structured in ways that will allow them to use their strengths and compensate for their specific learning difficulties. Ways in which lesson and

unit plans have been adapted for specific students should be documented. Make sure the learning need is defined and clearly addressed. This artifact could document your skills in meeting individual needs, your instructional strategies skills, and/or your knowledge of child development.

Interviews with Students, Teachers, Parents
These include planned conversations with a specific agenda. Include a copy of the questions and answers, as well as a summary and analysis of the interview. This interview may be part of a case study for one of your classes. Interviews can yield a variety of information; for example, an interview with a student may give you some indication of his or her language development, thus documenting your understanding of human development.

Journals
You may have kept journals during field classes or observation assignments. Include them if they address your observations of students as they relate to the desired standard. If necessary, highlight the appropriate sections of the journals. Make sure dates and times are included, but not the names of schools or teachers visited.

Lesson Plans
Copies of your lesson plans should include all components of a workable plan: objectives, materials, introduction, development, closing, and evaluation.

Sometimes plans may be used for more than one standard. In this case, highlight the specific part of the plan that documents the standard. Your ability to execute instructional planning and to use a variety of instructional strategies will be most obviously documented with lesson plans; however, it is possible that knowledge of content, use of environments and materials, communication skills, and knowledge of human development could be documented here.

Letters to Parents
Include copies of correspondence that you sent home. This could include permission slips, weekly newsletters, requests for parental help with homework, notices about parties, notification about field

trips, requests for parent conferences, student award certificates, or letters that explain upcoming activities. Such correspondence could document your cooperation with the home and community. Make sure letters contain correct spelling and standard English grammar.

Management and Organization Strategies

After trying a particular management or classroom organization strategy, systematically observe and code the events that occurred. This will enable you to record what is important about your experience. Write a brief summary and explanation of your observation. For example, you may have tried a chart system for classroom jobs, a record-keeping device for holistic scoring of writing, a system of recording anecdotal notes, or a way to expedite peer editing during writing classes. These types of explanations reflect your ability to manage the classroom well.

Media Competency

This type of document includes evidence and descriptions of the various forms of media you are able to incorporate in your instruction. This could include teaching resources such as the slide projector, camcorder and VCR, overhead projector, 16mm projector, computers and printers, interactive video, laser disks, and cable and electronic (educational) television.

You will also want to include evidence of your ability to incorporate technology into the classroom. Examples of how you have used e-mail, remote data bases, and distance learning equipment to research and to communicate with students and colleagues regionally, nationally, and internationally should be highlighted. A printout or floppy disk of your Internet address(es), listing of professional on-line "news group" and "listserve" memberships you hold, and examples of printed texts will provide documentation of your ability to share and retrieve information via the Internet.

Media competency reflects your ability to utilize a wide range of communication resources, environments, and materials appropriately. Therefore, you may wish to include a checklist of the various media and other "state-of-the-art" technology you are able to incorporate into your classroom.

Meetings and Workshops Log
If you have attended meetings or listened to speakers who discussed a topic related to a standard, include a reaction paper, plus a copy of the program. These logs would be a good way to document your professional commitment and responsibility.

Observation Reports
Systematic, regular noticing and recording of behaviors, events, and interactions in the classroom should be a part of every field experience you have. Include brief descriptions of your observations in a variety of grade levels. Reports could be in paragraph or checklist format. Depending upon the focus of your observations, your reports may reflect your knowledge of a variety of standards.

Peer Critiques
This encompasses formal and informal assessments of you by your fellow classmates. This could include score reports that are made out by classmates during your class presentations. The standard that you document with this artifact depends upon the presentation that your peers critique. If it was a lesson demonstration, your planning or instructional strategies skills would be evident. Your use of materials, communication skills, or knowledge of human development might also be evident. Make sure that the comments made by your peers reflect the standard that you are documenting.

Philosophy Statement
This is a brief position paper or statement of your philosophy of teaching. Make it clear and concrete. We recommend that you preface your entire portfolio with this statement. Sometimes it is an assignment in a class, but if not, write one on your own. It should include your underlying beliefs about the teaching strategies and practices that are best for students. Either leave out or explain educational jargon; do not include such terms simply because they "sound good." If you include the philosophy statement in more than one section, highlight the part that pertains to the specific standard.

Pictures and Photographs
Include photographs that show active learning in progress, special projects, field trips, or artistic expressions that cannot be physically

included in this notebook because of size. Bulletin boards, puppets, learning centers, and trips to museums are just some of the many ideas and activities you may want to photograph.

Depending on the photograph, you could document a variety of standards. If it is of a field trip that you took to a professional meeting or conference, document your professional commitment. If it is of a field trip or other related activity in which you participated with a class of students, you may want to document your use of instructional strategies, depending on your involvement in the planning process.

Portfolio (Student)
A student portfolio is an organized collection of a child's work that demonstrates the student's achievement and performance over time. Various kinds of evidence might be used, including the student's projects, written work, learning journals, and video demonstrations. A sample student portfolio would document your ability to use a variety of assessment strategies.

Position Papers
Include scholarly papers that were written to present an educational issue, viewpoint, or controversy. Be sure that sources are up to date. (No source should go back more than 5 years.) Papers such as these could document your professional commitment, as well as your knowledge of philosophical and social influences.

Problem-Solving Logs
As you identify professional problems or challenges, record them. It would be helpful to include a clear statement of the problem, alternative strategies for dealing with the problem, the chosen strategies, and the results of the implementation of each of them. Depending on the problem that you solved, you can document your use of instructional strategies, classroom management skills, or your cooperation with the home and community.

Professional Development Plans
Include a short paragraph or list explaining your short- and long-term plans for professional development. This could include efforts to improve knowledge or performance in specific areas of teaching,

attendance and participation in professional organizations or workshops, and plans for earning additional credits in graduate school. This area should reflect where you are now in terms of your profession and where you plan to be within the next few years. Such statements document your professional commitment and responsibility.

Professional Organizations and Committees List

List and briefly describe your involvement with an organization, committee, or other group that you feel has had an impact on you professionally or personally. Examples could include participation in campus and community organizations. Be sure to include some sort of evidence of your participation in these groups, such as a membership card, a letter of acceptance, or a program from an activity. Such memberships show that you actively seek out opportunities to grow professionally.

Professional Readings List

Keep a list of professional readings that you have done and include your reactions to the issues and concepts discussed. Your professional commitment and responsibility are reflected in professional reading lists.

Projects

Projects can include any type of assignment that involved problem solving, group presentations, creating materials, investigating phenomena in classrooms, or researching current information. In a presentation portfolio include paper copies only and make photographs of anything too large to fit in a notebook. If this is a group project, make that clear, but indicate the extent of your input. (Be careful about this one; it is not helpful to brag about "doing all the work"!)

The documentation possibilities of this artifact depend on the project. Examine the standards to determine if the project reflects instructional planning skills, professional commitment, the ability to meet individual needs, or knowledge of content.

References

References might include statements and/or evaluations from your supervisors of your academic work, experiences in the classroom, other work experience with children, or outside employment.

Try to connect the reference with one of your selected standards. For instance, the reference might describe a lesson you taught in a field course or in student teaching. Therefore, you could use this document to illustrate your competence in the area of multiple instructional strategies. In addition, you may want to place reference letters from your cooperating teachers in a special tabbed section of the notebook.

Research Papers
When selecting a research paper to include in your portfolio, you will need to consider several factors. The content of the research paper might make it appropriate for inclusion under a particular standard. It might, for instance, highlight your knowledge of an academic subject.

Rules and Procedures Descriptions
While you were student teaching or perhaps during field classes, you may have had the opportunity to write your own classroom rules or procedures. This document should describe the regular, repeated guidelines or routines for behavior that give your classroom predictability and order. These descriptions of rules should give some evidence of your ability to manage the classroom and create an environment conducive to learning and positive interaction.

Schedules
During student teaching you were probably asked to complete a daily schedule. If you use this as a document, be sure that it clearly describes your format for the events of the day for students under your supervision. The order of events and the length of time allotted to each should be clear and concise. Classroom management skills are reflected in this type of artifact.

Seating Arrangement Diagrams
A particular seating arrangement (such as having students sit in groups) might complement a particular teaching strategy (such as cooperative learning). It might also reflect a particular classroom management need, such as having students seated apart from the rest of the class. Your ability to plan for instruction, use environments, and manage the classroom could be documented with this artifact.

Self-Assessment Instruments
This includes results from instruments, rating scales, surveys, or questionnaires that provide feedback about your performance. This shows your professional commitment and responsibility. Self-assessment instruments also include examples of instruments that you developed to engage students in measuring their own performance (cognitive, affective, and psychomotor). These could document your assessment skills.

Simulated Experiences
Include an explanation of educational experiences in which you learned through the use of simulation as a teaching method. A simulation is an activity that represents a real-life experience. This activity could include teaching an elementary lesson in a methods class, dramatizing a simulated classroom management scenario, or some other type of role-play experience. Describe the simulation, its purpose, and what you feel you learned from the experience. The simulation itself will determine the standard that you can document here.

Student Contracts
You may have the opportunity to write individual (one-on-one) contracts to help promote a student's academic achievement or improved behavior. The actual "contract" should look formal—it should be typed and should specifically spell out the conditions under which the terms of the contract (achievement, behavior, etc.) will be met. In addition, it should include a space for the teacher and the student to sign, date, and confirm their agreement to the conditions. You may not have the need to draw up contracts until you student teach, but you may see some in use during your field experiences. (Classroom management rules that all students are expected to follow do not qualify under this category.) This type of artifact reflects your ability to develop learning experiences on the basis of diagnosis and observation, or perhaps it can document your classroom management skills, depending on the reason for the individual contract.

Subscriptions

If you subscribe to a journal that specifically addresses the standard in its title, include a copy of the cover of the journal, along with the address label showing your name. You might also briefly mention any ideas, instructional techniques, or other helpful information you gathered from reading the journal. Generally, professional commitment is well documented with subscriptions; however, you may find other standards to document with this artifact, depending on the type of journal to which you subscribe.

Teacher-Made Materials

These materials may include games, manipulatives, puppets, big books, charts, videotapes, films, photographs, transparencies, teaching aids, costumes, posters, or artwork. Because many of these items are cumbersome, include only paper copies or photographs of the materials. If you do not have copies of the actual materials that you have made, you may want to highlight sections of a well-designed lesson plan that show how you would use some creative teaching materials. Materials that support learning theory and were designed to suit this purpose are most helpful. Your materials should reflect your ability to encourage active learning and a variety of instructional strategies.

Theme Studies

This is a set of lesson plans or resource materials that fit a central theme. Theme studies integrate many subjects, which might include math, science, health, physical education, English, social studies, reading, art, music, and spelling. Make sure that your plans contain all elements of good lesson plans and are obviously related to your overall theme. Your knowledge of a variety of instructional strategies should be evident through your use of computer programs, children's literature, manipulatives, films, charts, or concrete materials. In addition, your instructional planning skills will be evident.

Transcripts

A copy of your official transcript can be used in a variety of ways. You may wish to use it to document your knowledge in subject areas such as chemistry or geography or in education courses.

Highlight the courses and the grade you wish to document. Include a brief, typewritten explanation of why this transcript is included. You may even include other information such as a syllabus from the course you have highlighted, to show that you have taken essay or other types of tests on the subject.

Unit Plans

A unit plan is an integrated plan for instruction on a topic that is developed over several days or even weeks. Often units are developed within a discipline and lessons are organized so as to build on knowledge acquired in previous lessons. Unit plans generally include purposes, objectives, content outlines, activities, instructional resources, and evaluation methods. (Interdisciplinary units have been described under the entry called Theme Studies.) Unit plans are particularly good for documenting your ability to use a variety of instructional strategies and instructional planning skills.

Video Scenario Critiques

Often in college methods courses, professors will ask you to view and critique a videotape of actual teaching scenarios. If you wish to include a critique that you have completed, be sure to describe the scenario and give its bibliographical information. Make sure the critique speaks to the standard you plan to document. Depending on the nature of the video, there are several possibilities for documentation.

Volunteer Experiences Descriptions

This document might include a list and brief description of volunteer experiences and services provided to the school and community. You should focus on how these activities have enhanced your abilities while providing a contribution to society. You should also emphasize the importance of maintaining positive school–community collaboration through teacher, parent, and student interaction. Depending on what you learned from these experiences, make sure they address the standard under which you have placed this document.

Work Experience Descriptions

These are statements that you have written to describe work experiences. These might include work with students in both traditional and nontraditional settings and work for which you were either compensated or that you performed on a voluntary basis. To be of most interest, these statements should include not only a summary of the setting and your responsibilities, but also a reflective statement addressing the intangible aspects of the work experience. In writing these statements, be sure to show how these work experiences relate to the specific standard.

APPENDIX C

Rubrics to Use in a Portfolio Checkpoint System

RUBRIC FOR PORTFOLIO EVALUATION: SOPHOMORE CHECKPOINT

Exceptional Rating

- The portfolio contains one of each of the documents listed below, plus at least one additional document of any type.
  - A. One performance assessment task from the entry-level introduction to teaching course
  - B. One self-selected document
  - C. One self-generated document

- Documents are appropriate for chosen standards.
- Rationales describe the document clearly and concisely in terms that can be understood by a general audience.
- Rationales are convincing and clearly explain why the documents meet the standards.
- Self-reflection in specific terms is evident in the document as well as in the cover sheet. Reflections address both strengths and needs for improvement.

- There are no mechanical errors throughout the portfolio.
- All necessary revisions have been made.
- The portfolio makes a visual impact, with use of photos, graphics, illustrations, and artwork.

Acceptable Rating

- The portfolio contains the number of documents listed below.
  A. One performance assessment task from the entry-level introduction to teaching course
  B. One self-selected document
  C. One self-generated document
- Documents are appropriate for chosen standards.
- Rationales describe the document clearly and concisely.
- Rationales adequately explain the value of the document to the student's professional growth.
- Rationales show self-reflection in specific terms.
- Documents and rationales are well edited.
- The portfolio has an overall professional appearance.

Not Acceptable Rating

- Any of the types of documents listed below are missing from the portfolio.
  A. One performance assessment task from the entry-level introduction to teaching course
  B. One self-selected document
  C. One self-generated document
- Documents are misfiled.
- Rationales inadequately describe documents.
- Rationales give limited insight into the student's professional growth.
- Mechanical errors interfere with the student's purpose.
- Further revisions are required on documents.
- The portfolio exhibits inadequate organization and lacks professional appearance.

RUBRIC FOR PORTFOLIO EVALUATION: JUNIOR CHECKPOINT

Exceptional Rating

- The portfolio contains the number of documents listed below, plus at least one additional document of any type.
  - A. One performance assessment task from each professional methods course taken
  - B. Three self-selected documents
  - C. Three self-generated documents

- Documents are appropriate for chosen standards.
- Rationales describe the document clearly and concisely in terms that can be understood by a general audience.
- Rationales are convincing and clearly explain why the documents meet the standards.
- Self-reflection in specific terms is evident in the document as well as in the cover sheet. Reflections address both strengths and needs for improvement.
- There are no mechanical errors throughout the portfolio.
- All necessary revisions have been made.
- The portfolio makes a visual impact, with use of photos, graphics, illustrations, and artwork.
- The portfolio reflects work with the entire age range for which the student will be certified.

Acceptable Rating

- The portfolio contains the number of documents listed below.
  - A. One performance assessment task from each professional methods course taken
  - B. Three self-selected documents
  - C. Three self-generated documents

- Documents are appropriate for chosen standards.
- Rationales describe the document clearly and concisely.
- Rationales adequately explain the value of the document to the student's professional growth.

- Rationales show self-reflection in specific terms.
- Documents and rationales are well edited.
- The portfolio has an overall professional appearance.
- The portfolio reflects work with the entire age range for which the student will be certified.

Not Acceptable Rating

- Less than any of the numbers listed below are contained in the portfolio.
  A. One performance assessment task from each professional methods course taken
  B. Three self-selected documents
  C. Three self-generated documents

- Documents are misfiled.
- Rationales inadequately describe documents.
- Rationales give limited insight into the student's professional growth.
- Mechanical errors interfere with the student's purpose.
- Further revisions are required on documents.
- The portfolio exhibits inadequate organization and lacks professional appearance.
- The portfolio reflects work with only part of the age group for which the student will be certified.

RUBRIC FOR PORTFOLIO EVALUATION: SENIOR CHECKPOINT

Exceptional Rating

- The portfolio contains the number of documents listed below, plus at least one additional document of any type.
  - A. One performance assessment task from each professional methods course taken
  - B. Six self-selected documents
  - C. Six self-generated documents
- Each standard has two or more documents.
- Documents are appropriate for chosen standards.
- Rationales describe the document clearly and concisely in terms that can be understood by a general audience.
- Rationales are convincing and clearly explain why the documents meet the standards.
- Self-reflection in specific terms is evident in the document as well as in the cover sheet. Reflections address both strengths and needs for improvement.
- There are no mechanical errors throughout the portfolio.
- All necessary revisions have been made.
- The portfolio makes a visual impact, with use of photos, graphics, illustrations, and artwork.
- The portfolio reflects work with the entire age range for which the student will be certified.

Acceptable Rating

- The portfolio contains the number of documents listed below.
  - A. One performance assessment task from each professional methods course taken
  - B. Six self-selected documents
  - C. Six self-generated documents
- Most standards have two documents; all have at least one document.
- Documents are appropriate for chosen standards.

- Rationales describe the document clearly and concisely.
- Rationales adequately explain the value of the document to the student's professional growth.
- Rationales show self-reflection in specific terms.
- Documents and rationales are well edited.
- The portfolio has an overall professional appearance.
- The portfolio reflects work with the entire age range for which the student will be certified.

Not Acceptable Rating

- Less than any of the numbers listed below are contained in the portfolio.
  A. One performance assessment task from each professional methods course taken
  B. Six self-selected documents
  C. Six self-generated documents

- Fewer than half the standards have two documents or not all standards have a document.
- Documents are misfiled.
- Rationales inadequately describe documents.
- Rationales give limited insight into the student's professional growth.
- Mechanical errors interfere with the student's purpose.
- Further revisions are required on documents.
- The portfolio exhibits inadequate organization and lacks professional appearance.
- The portfolio reflects work with only part of the age group for which the student will be certified.

APPENDIX D

Self-Assessment Sorting Exercise for Determining Values in Teaching

SORTING INSTRUCTIONS TO PRE-SERVICE TEACHERS

You have been given a set of behavioral indicators, which were written by faculty members, elementary school teachers, and students. They contain statements about the kinds of skills, teaching behaviors, and dispositions that reflect the ten standards that have been adopted by our department. This self-assessment activity will help you to reflect upon the experiences you have had and to clarify your values related to these program standards. Thus, after completing this sorting activity, you will be able to review your portfolio documents in relationship to your values. In addition, this sorting activity will be a valuable tool, functioning as a springboard for conferencing with your advisor and setting goals for yourself as you prepare to begin student teaching. Please do the following:

1. Divide the stack into three piles with fifteen cards per pile. The right-hand pile indicates skills or attitudes that you most value. The center pile indicates those that you value second in importance. The left-hand pile will indicate those that you value as third in importance to you.
2. From the right-hand pile, pull out five statements to which you give priority and put those five to your extreme right. From the left-hand pile, pull out five statements to which you give the lowest priority and put these five to your extreme left. There should now be five piles. The pile on the extreme right has five cards, the next pile has ten, the middle pile has fifteen, the next pile has ten, and the extreme left pile contains five cards.
3. Each pile is assigned a number, starting on the left. The extreme left pile is assigned the number 1, then the next pile is assigned a number 2, the next pile is a 3, the next pile is a 4, and the last pile is assigned a number 5.
4. Use the Self-Assessment Values Summary Chart (Table D.1) to record these piles. For each pile, record the number on the card in its appropriate pile number column on the chart.
5. Now you need to transpose your pile numbers to the Values Scoring Chart (Table D.2), to determine the standard(s) that you value most. On this chart, in each Standard Column, you will see five card numbers listed. These cards are associated with that standard. Next to the card number, put your pile number in the blank. (For example, if card #4 was placed in your pile #3, put a 3 next to the 4 under Standard #10 for Partnerships.)
6. After listing all the numbers, add each pile column. The column with the highest total indicates the standard you value the most; the column with the lowest total indicates the standard you value the least.
7. On the Self-Assessment Values Summary Chart, write at least one academic or professional goal, based on the standards for teaching that you value the most.

**TABLE D.1   Chart Used for Summarizing Self-Assessment
Sorting Activity**

Self-Assessment Values Summary Chart

Name: _____ Date of Junior Checkpoint Interview: _____

After sorting your cards according to instructions, record their corresponding
numbers here. Determine your values by matching the numbers in Pile #5 to the
chart that shows the standards they most closely reflect.

PILE #1	PILE #2	PILE #3	PILE #4	PILE #5
XXXXXXXXX				XXXXXXXXX
XXXXXXXXX				XXXXXXXXX
XXXXXXXXX				XXXXXXXXX
XXXXXXXXX				XXXXXXXXX
XXXXXXXXX				XXXXXXXXX
XXXXXXXXX	XXXXXXXXX		XXXXXXXXX	XXXXXXXXX
XXXXXXXXX	XXXXXXXXX		XXXXXXXXX	XXXXXXXXX
XXXXXXXXX	XXXXXXXXX		XXXXXXXXX	XXXXXXXXX
XXXXXXXXX	XXXXXXXXX		XXXXXXXXX	XXXXXXXXX
XXXXXXXXX	XXXXXXXXX		XXXXXXXXX	XXXXXXXXX

Goal(s) based on my values: _____

_____

_____

_____

TABLE D.2 Values Sorting Activity Scoring Chart

Values Scoring Chart

Standard #2, Human Development & Learning	Standard #3, Individual Needs	Standard #4, Multiple Instructional Strategies	Standard #5, Classroom Motivation & Management
Card # Pile #	Card # Pile #	Card # Pile #	Card # Pile #
11	10	6	1
14	13	19	20
30	32	25	34
35	41	28	36
44	43	37	45
Total:	Total:	Total:	Total:

Standard #6, Communication Skills	Standard #7, Instructional Planning Skills	Standard #8, Assessment	Standard #9, Professional Commitment & Responsibility	Standard #10, Partnerships
Card # Pile #	Card # Pile #	Card # Pile #	Card # Pile #	Card # Pile #
2	8	3	9	4
5	18	7	17	12
29	22	16	21	15
31	27	24	23	38
42	33	39	26	40
Total:	Total:	Total:	Total:	Total:

Note: Standard #1 is not included due to the wide variety of subject matter that it addresses.

BEHAVIORAL INDICATORS TO USE
IN THE VALUES SORT EXERCISE

1. The teacher utilizes various teaching strategies that encourage both individual and group involvement.
2. The teacher uses discussion techniques that are conducive to higher thinking skills.
3. The teacher adjusts success-rate expectations for individual children to be appropriately challenging.
4. The teacher promotes a spirit of collaboration, collegiality and personal growth in the school.
5. The teacher uses standard English oral and written grammar, avoiding slang and colloquial expressions.
6. The teacher utilizes inductive and deductive teaching strategies.
7. The teacher assists the children to assess their own learning in child portfolios.
8. The teacher recognizes dissonance between personal and philosophical orientation and curriculum restraints and is able to adapt as the need arises.
9. The teacher reads professional journals in the field.
10. The teacher accommodates differences through a variety of instructional strategies.
11. The teacher engages in "kid watching," (i.e., verbal and non-verbal signals from students) on a daily basis.
12. The teacher engages in volunteer activities that enhance the local community.
13. The teacher matches teaching method to student learning style.
14. The teacher provides information and support around students' irrational fears, anxieties, and frustrational levels.
15. The teacher utilizes services of local agencies in planning.
16. The teacher, through assessment, can help students build a realistic sense of self-worth to take into the world.
17. The teacher collaborates with other teachers to create materials and strategies.
18. The teacher demonstrates some flexibility in philosophical orientation.
19. The teacher uses cooperative learning techniques to promote learning through socialization and collaboration.

20. The teacher establishes a classroom design that enables the students to take advantage of various learning experiences.
21. The teacher attends inservice meetings, workshops, conferences, and PTA meetings.
22. The teacher recognizes that different teaching strategies will have direct effects on student behavior.
23. The teacher writes self-evaluative statements after and/or while teaching a lesson.
24. The teacher assesses student interaction and social development through informal observations.
25. The teacher selects manipulatives that help in the child's construction of knowledge.
26. The teacher develops a professional portfolio that demonstrates self-reflection.
27. The teacher develops a philosophy of teaching.
28. The teacher engages students in demonstrating the cognitive levels of application, analysis, and synthesis.
29. The teacher uses audio-visual media to develop conceptual knowledge.
30. The teacher provides meaningful projects that enhance development.
31. The teacher integrates computer-based instructional materials or methods into a lesson.
32. The teacher demonstrates awareness of individual student differences and needs.
33. The teacher develops meaningful lesson plans utilizing a variety of teaching strategies.
34. The teacher allows students to interact with their peers and take responsibility for their learning.
35. The teacher recognizes that each child develops at his or her own rate.
36. The teacher provides appropriate problem-solving strategies in social and academic situations.
37. The teacher demonstrates the link between conceptual knowledge and procedural knowledge by utilizing discovery teaching methods.
38. The teacher provides opportunities for parent involvement.

39. The teacher assesses children with special needs in unique and appropriate ways, maximizing their strengths.

40. The teacher utilizes the school and community resources to meet the needs of students with diverse backgrounds (rural, urban, racial, cultural).

41. The teacher demonstrates awareness of age characteristics.

42. The teacher creates challenging and appropriate bulletin boards, classroom displays, and learning centers that promote critical thinking, problem solving and creativity.

43. The teacher modifies the classroom environment to meet the needs of all students.

44. The teacher writes appropriate performance objectives for projects and activities.

45. The teacher organizes the classroom activities with a sense of predictability.

Transcript of a Sample Junior Checkpoint Conference

Patti Baxter has completed 88 credits and is a dual major in elementary and early childhood education. She has completed her junior checkpoint advisement forms, Self-Assessment of Values Summary, and Artifacts Checklist. She turned those in, along with her portfolio, to the Elementary Education office 3 days ago. Her junior checkpoint conference is scheduled for this afternoon at 2:00 with Dr. Nancy Smith.

Dr. Smith: Hi, Patti! You're right on time. Come in and have a seat.

Patti: Thanks! (Patti sits in a chair next to Dr. Smith's desk.)

Dr. Smith: I've looked at your junior checkpoint advisement forms. It seems that you've completed all the necessary requirements up to this point. That QPA is nice—3.7! Good for you!

Patti: Thanks. I've been working really hard to keep my grades up.

Dr. Smith: I can tell. So, let's see, the NTE score is here, and your field experiences are done.

Patti: That's right.

Dr. Smith: Here's the list of courses that you'll need to finish before you student teach. Are you aware of all of these? If so, you'll need to sign this list.

(Patti looks over the list and compares it with her distribution sheet. She signs on the designated line to indicate her agreement that the list is accurate.)

Patti: Yes, this looks like it's right. I've got fourteen classes to go before I student teach next year. I've registered for five of these this spring, and I hope to pick up four in the summer. Then, I'll have five more next fall and I'll student teach next spring!

Dr. Smith: Great! OK, I'd like to ask you just a couple of questions. I notice that you took Instructional Strategies last year and that you've had a few of our methods courses. I'm sure that you've heard of the constructivist philosophy, am I right?

Patti: I certainly have!

Dr. Smith: Can you tell me the role of the teacher in the constructivist philosophy?

Patti: Sure. From what I understand, the teacher is a facilitator.

Dr. Smith: Tell me more. What does it mean to facilitate?

Patti: Well, the teacher knows what it is that she wants the students to learn and guides them to that outcome. She doesn't just tell them the information. Instead, she uses questions, modeling, discussions, and materials to help the students find out for themselves what they need to know.

Dr. Smith: Is what the teacher deems important the only thing the students need to know?

Patti: Oh, no. The constructivist teacher also wants to teach children strategies for learning more about topics that interest them, because that is intrinsically motivating to them.

Dr. Smith: I think you've got a good handle on that! Now, here's your portfolio. I've had a chance to look over it and am impressed with the documents that you have included. Could you point out one document that reflects constructivism?

Patti: Hmm, let me look for a second. (Patti peruses her portfolio for just a minute, then points out a document.) Here's one. It's a lesson plan that I wrote and put under Standard #7. I wrote it for my Language and Literacy class, and it shows how I taught some vocabulary to my fifth-grade field class.

Dr. Smith: And how is this constructivist?

Patti: Well, as you can see, I used some strategies that helped the students understand the meanings of these words in a concrete way, such as role-playing and sharing personal experiences. I asked some questions that helped them to see that each of the words had different meanings for different contexts.

Dr. Smith: Do you see yourself as a facilitator in this lesson?

Patti: Absolutely!

Dr. Smith: Why?

Patti: Well, because I didn't just tell them the meanings of these words, and I didn't just ask them to look them up in the dictionary. Instead, I used these questions, which led the students to the conclusion.

Dr. Smith: I agree with you. Your choice of questions is appropriate for a constructivist lesson. And I see from your Sophomore Checkpoint Form that you wrote a goal at that time: "I will write questions that lead to discovery in my lesson plans." I think you met that goal quite well. What do you think?

Patti: Oh, I agree. It's hard to get children to see something for themselves without actually telling them the answer, but I'm working on it!

Dr. Smith: Good for you. Now, I had the chance to look at two of your self-generated documents and two of your self-selected documents. Let's see, let me find one. (She looks for a self-generated document.) Ah, here it is. You attended the Gender Bias in Education Panel Discussion here on campus and wrote your reaction. I notice that you filed this under Standard #9. Why?

Patti: Well, because I think it shows that I put forth a little bit of extra effort to learn more about my profession. I found out a lot of things I didn't know about gender biases in the classroom. For example, I never realized that teachers usually call on boys more often. After the meeting I made a conscious effort to pay attention to who I called on in my field classes. I think the meeting was a very enlightening one, because it opened a lot of people's eyes.

Dr. Smith: I agree with you. Let's look at your rationale. It does a wonderful job of summarizing the panel discussion. Explaining the value of an experience is also important. Do you think you could make it explain exactly what you just told me? That way, your rationale will also do a great job of explaining how the meeting was important to your professional growth.

Patti: That makes sense. Yeah, I'll try that.

Dr. Smith: Great. Now, looking at the other documents that you chose to put in this portfolio, and at your Artifacts Checklist, I noticed that you filed both of your self-generated ones under Standard #9, Professional Commitment, and both of your self-selected ones under Standard #7, Instructional Planning Skills. Can you tell me why?

Patti: Well, the self-generated ones show things that I did outside of class, and I thought that would reflect on my professionalism. The self-selected ones were my best lesson plans, and I wanted to use them in my portfolio.

Dr. Smith: I see. Your lesson plans are indeed excellent. Since you already have two other lesson plans under that same standard, could you place them somewhere else?

Patti: Gee, I don't know. They show my planning skills pretty well.

Dr. Smith: You're absolutely right. Let's look at this one in particular. (She points to a plan.) In this plan you did a fine job of using developmentally appropriate activities for first-graders. I notice that you were very careful to use personal experiences and concrete objects when explaining concepts to young children in this social studies lesson. Is there a standard that states that you understand how children learn and develop and that you can plan for that?

Patti: (Thinks for a minute, then looks through her portfolio.) Yes, isn't it Standard #2?

Dr. Smith: That's right. Could you put at least one of your lesson plans there?

Patti: Yeah, I think I could. And I don't have anything filed there yet!

Dr. Smith: That's right. Yet you seem to understand child development very well.

Patti: Thanks.

Dr. Smith: Now, looking at your Self-Assessment of Values Summary, I see that you value the ability to adapt instruction for individual needs. Your application for admission to teacher education also shows a goal that you wrote: "I want to be able to write lesson plans that meet the needs of all the students in my class."

Patti: I sure do. I think it's absolutely imperative that teachers meet all the needs of all the children.

Dr. Smith: You're right. How can teachers do this?

Patti: Well, first of all, they have to know the children. They need to know what the children can do, what they like, and how they like to learn. This will help them understand how to help children do things that they are not so strong in.

Dr. Smith: Can you give me an example?

Patti: Let me think. Well, there was a student in my first-grade field class—Joshua. He was really interested in dinosaurs. But he couldn't read well. I think the teacher may be able to reach him a bit more if she provides dinosaur books for him. Even if he can't read every single word, he will still be getting information from pictures, charts, and captions. And he'll be more motivated to read the hard parts.

Dr. Smith: You've shown a lot of insight. What can you do to document what you just told me?

Patti: Well, my cooperating teacher has invited me to come back anytime. Maybe I could go back and offer to tutor him, and use some of my ideas.

Dr. Smith: Excellent idea. Will you have time?

Patti: Gee, I don't know. I'm taking a full load of classes.

Dr. Smith: Well, do any of your professors ask you to do outside projects?

Patti: Yes, Dr. Jones offers bonus points for stuff like that. And Dr. Collins requires that all students do a service project.

Dr. Smith: Hmm. Maybe you could meet your goal and document Standard #3 by doing some work with Joshua for one of those classes.

Patti: Yeah! I think I can work that out.

Dr. Smith: Great! Well, I think we've covered everything. We need to check off this conference form. You had the appropriate number of documents in your portfolio. You are going to do a little bit of revision on the documents that we talked about and the rationale for the gender bias panel. From looking through your portfolio the last couple of days, I have found that you have given it an overall professional appearance and have edited your documents well. As do most of our students, you have prepared a portfolio that is acceptable, and I will rate it as such on this form. After you make these few revisions and seek opportunities to document Standard #3, I feel sure that your portfolio is well on its way to an "exceptional" rating. And I think you will be able to meet your own goal, too.

Patti: Thanks so much!

Glossary

Artifact   Tangible evidence that indicates the attainment of knowledge and skills and the ability to apply understandings to complex tasks. Examples include professional work samples, videos, letters, class assignments, student products, or certificates.

Artifacts Checklist   Checklist of artifacts or documents students begin during the sophomore-level checkpoint. Students mark the artifacts included in their portfolios. As students progress through the program, the checklist provides a current inventory of the contents of the portfolio. (See Appendix A.)

Authentic Assessment   A performance assessment that measures students' abilities to apply their understanding in authentic contexts. To do this, students are given assignments that involve real-world problem solving. These are tasks that are frequently performed by inservice professionals and serve a real purpose in a real-life situation.

Behavioral Indicators   Specific performance behaviors that collectively provide a more complete description of what a standard looks like in practice.

Behaviorism   A prominent school of thought about learning and teaching that focuses on why people behave as they do and how to shape their behavior. Those advocating behaviorism rely most often on the direct teaching of content considered valuable by the culture.

Celebration Workshop   A workshop in which student teachers showcase their portfolios to members of the university community and public school teachers and administrators.

Checkpoints   A system for monitoring program goals and attainment of standards. Checkpoints are conducted during interviews between a faculty member and student during the sophomore, junior, and senior years. The purposes of checkpoints are threefold: (1) to ascertain that program requirements are being met, (2) to have students present and discuss their portfolio with a faculty advisor, and (3) to ensure a growing understanding of the program philosophy.

Constructivism   A school of thought about learning and teaching that maintains that students gain deep understanding of content only when they act on information by integrating it with prior knowledge. Those advocating constructivism rely heavily upon indirect and cooperative approaches to teaching content that the students find valuable.

Continuum of Performance Assessments   A way of visualizing performance assessments in terms of their purpose. On one end of the continuum are assignments that assess discrete, discernible skills that must be evaluated alone, which may be used to determine the student's readiness to move on to a broader assignment or to assess an important goal in detail. On the other end of the continuum are assignments that reflect a wider range of abilities, which are used to integrate a variety of skills and knowledge or focus on the creation of a whole product. Projects or tasks can fall anywhere on this continuum, depending on their complexity, scope, and purpose.

Cooperating Teacher   A master teacher from the school site who supports and facilitates the student teachers' and field students' classroom experiences. The cooperating teacher's role includes observation, supervision, and assessment of the preservice teachers' performance. Cooperating teachers also collaborate with university faculty on improvements in clinical experiences for preservice teachers.

Course-Embedded Performance Assessments   Performance assessment projects or tasks that are assigned in a course that is required in the program. By requiring such performances in all courses in the teacher education program, faculty can be reasonably sure that program standards are being taught and met.

Cover Sheet   The page that precedes a portfolio entry, created for the purpose of orienting a reader to the artifact and its relevance.

Curriculum Map   A summary that indicates the overall picture of the content, skills, and/or assessments being provided in an education program, which is prepared in order to facilitate communication and curriculum decision making.

Discrete Performances   Student behaviors that are specific and show capabilities to perform single or a very few objectives or standards.

Enabling Model of Performance Assessment   A supportive approach to portfolio work in which the focus is on continuous improvement, goal setting, and showing what a candidate can do in actual practice.

Focus-Oriented Courses   Courses that are designed to address a specific issue in depth and at length. Such courses usually require a comprehensive performance assessment project, assess inclusive or holistic learning, and address a variety of objectives, standards, or outcomes.

Inclusive Performances   Student behaviors that reflect capabilities in several objectives or standards and show the results of holistic learning.

Interstate New Teacher Assessment and Support Consortium (INTASC)   A consortium of more than thirty states operating under the Council of Chief State School Officials that has developed standards and an assessment process for initial teacher certification.

INTASC Standards   A set of expectations applicable for beginning teachers of all disciplines and grade levels developed by the Interstate New Teacher Assessment and Support Consortium.

Mentor   An upperclassman who provides reliable information, support, and guidance to incoming students. The mentor facilitates transition into the program under the direction of department staff and university advisors.

National Board for Professional Teaching Standards   A board created to achieve two primary purposes: (1) to develop standards in many fields for what accomplished teachers should know and be able to do and (2) to develop a voluntary national credential for accomplished teachers that includes the presentation of portfolios based on these standards.

National Commission on Teaching and America's Future   A commission funded by the Rockefeller Foundation and Carnegie Corporation of New York to consider policies and practices that will ensure higher student achievement and more effective teaching.

National Council for Accreditation of Teacher Education (NCATE)   A coalition of thirty-three specialty professional associations of teachers, teacher educators, content specialists, and local and state policymakers. NCATE is best known for its process of professional accreditation of schools, colleges, and departments of education.

NCATE 2000   A new performance-based system of accreditation in teacher education. Accreditation decisions will focus primarily on the performance of the institution and its candidates. More emphasis will be placed on the quality of candidate work, candidate subject matter knowledge, and demonstrated teaching skill.

Partnership Portfolio   A systematic collection of artifacts assembled around components of the Professional Development School. The Partnership Portfolio communicates the PDS philosophy and programs and provides evidence of accomplishment of program goals. The portfolio can be showcased by university and school district faculty during presentations at state and national conferences, support efforts to secure funding and grants, and serve as documentation during institution accreditations.

Peer Editing   Editing of a student's work that is done by another student or a peer outside the classroom. It is an important part of the process of completing the performance assessment task, because it requires students to make sure that their work clearly articulates their understandings for an audience other than the professor. This concept not only helps students improve their work, but it also models the real-life work of professionals.

Performance Assessment   A task or project that enables a student to demonstrate abilities to meet course objectives or standards. Such assessments require students to synthesize the knowledge, skills, and dispositions acquired in a course; reflect the real-life work of the profession; revise their written work; make choices that reflect their interests and needs; and reflect upon the professional value of the experience.

Performance Assessment Project   A type of performance assessment that synthesizes all or a large part of the learning that has taken place in a course. Usually such assignments are designed to take an entire semester to complete and are the sole product of the course. They assess the students' abilities to perform all or most of the objectives and desired outcomes of the course; thus, they reflect inclusive learning. Several program standards can be met with this type of project. Examples of projects include case studies, theme boxes, and units.

Performance Assessment Summary   A compilation of all performance assessments used in the program, including a description of the tasks or projects, behavioral indicators connecting the tasks or projects to specific program standards, and examples of the tasks or projects produced by students. The summary is used for program self-evaluation, to determine whether certain types of artifacts are being overused, and to ascertain whether there is an overemphasis on some standards while others are minimally addressed.

Performance Assessment Task   A type of performance assessment that reflects a limited number of course objectives or outcomes and, most often, only one program standard. Tasks are valuable because they authentically assess learning on some important aspect of the course. They require discrete performances by students. Examples of tasks include lesson plan components, memos or letters, position papers, and journal article critiques.

Philosophical Orientation   A cohesive conceptual framework that becomes a basis for applying theory to practice.

Portfolio (Professional)   An organized collection of complex, performance-based evidence that indicates one's growth, goals, and current knowledge and skills needed to be competent in a role or area of expertise.

Portfolio Assessment System   A process designed to assess changes over time in the growing competence and performance of students or practitioners through tangible evidence organized in portfolios.

Portfolio Day   A day during the mid-semester of student teaching when student teachers visit sophomore and junior university methods classes to share portfolio artifacts and rationales. Seniors discuss the multiple uses of the portfolio for designing and monitoring professional development.

Presentation Portfolio   A portfolio that is a carefully streamlined and organized collection of work samples and other pieces of evidence prepared to share with others, especially with those making judgments about one's achieved competence.

Professional Development School (PDS)   A collaborative learning community in which long-term professional growth and the development of relationships among and across teachers and university faculty are supported. PDS members work together to learn first-hand about different approaches to improving education for students and teachers. Preservice teachers trained at PDS sites interact in school-based activities supported by research and reflection grounded in university course work and portfolio standards.

Rationale   The part of a cover sheet for a portfolio entry that explains or justifies one's reasoning for the inclusion of a portfolio artifact. It summarizes the document and experience, explains their professional value, and describes implications for future work.

Reflection   The disciplined practice of considering the effects of one's own behavior and decisions on other people and on one's own development.

Rubric   A set of criteria and a scoring scale that is used to assess and evaluate students' work. Often rubrics identify levels or ranks with criteria indicated for each level. The rubrics used in a portfolio assessment system outline the quantity of documents needed in a portfolio and the quality of the connections between artifacts and standards. Rubrics guide students in setting goals, gaining autonomy over their own learning, and showcasing their strengths.

Self-Assessment of Values   An activity completed by students prior to the junior-level checkpoint. Students sort behavioral indicators into piles according to the kinds of skills or attitudes that they value. Based upon the results, students create academic and/or professional goals.

Self-Generated Documents   Artifacts that students create to document professional growth activities outside of class, such as volunteer work, independent reading, and attendance at professional conferences.

Self-Selected Documents   Assignments from any college credit course that students select to put into the portfolio because they value the learning that they provide.

Standards   Expected learning outcomes that delineate the key aspects of professional performance.

Survey-Oriented Courses   Courses that are designed to address a wide range of teaching skills and capabilities. These courses lend themselves to the assignment of performance assessment tasks which assess discrete performances and only one or a very few objectives, standards, or outcomes at a time.

University Supervisor   A university professor who supervises the student teacher's site assignments. The role of the university supervisor includes establishing appropriate assignments for student teachers, conducting observations, supervising and evaluating student teacher performance, conducting weekly practicum seminars, and organizing authentic experiences within and beyond the classroom.

Working Portfolio   A portfolio that is organized around standards and contains the complete collection of past work in unabridged form as well as work in progress. Often students maintain a working portfolio with a system of file folders that are labeled with standards. Work in progress is filed appropriately, then later revised and/or updated to be inserted in the presentation portfolio.

References

Arends, R. (1994). *Learning to teach*. New York: McGraw-Hill.

Association for Supervision and Curriculum Development (ASCD). (1997). *Developing performance assessments*. [Videotape.] Alexandria, VA: Author.

Barton, J., & Collins, A. (1993). Portfolios in teacher education. *Journal of Teacher Education, 44*(3), 200–211.

California Department of Education. (1997, July). *California standards for the teaching profession*. Sacramento: California Commission on Teacher Credentialing and The California Department of Education.

Campbell, D., Cignetti, P., Melenyzer, B., Nettles, D., & Wyman, R. (1994). *A constructivist model for teaching*. Unpublished manuscript, California University of Pennsylvania.

Campbell, D., Cignetti, P., Melenyzer, B., Nettles, D., & Wyman, R. (1997). *How to develop a professional portfolio: A manual for teachers*. Boston: Allyn and Bacon.

Cronin, J. (1993). Four misconceptions about authentic learning. *Educational Leadership, 50*(7),78–80.

Darling-Hammond, L. (Ed.). (1992, September). *Model standards for beginning teacher licensing and development*. Unpublished draft, Washington, DC: Interstate New Teacher Assessment and Support Consortium, and Council of Chief State School Officers.

Darling-Hammond, L. (1994). Developing professional development schools: Early lessons, challenges, and promise. In L. Darling-Hammond (Ed.), *Professional development schools*. New York: Teacher College Press.

Diez, M. E. (1997). The context for accountability. *AACTE Briefs, 18*(9), 6–7.

Diez, M. (1998). *Changing the practice of teacher education*. Washington, DC: American Association of Colleges for Teacher Education.

Diez, M., & Hass, J. (1997). No more piecemeal reform: Using performance-based approaches to rethink teacher education. *Action in Teacher Education, 19*(2), 17–26.

Diez, M., & Moon, C. J. (1992). What do we want students to know? And other important questions. *Educational Leadership, 49*(8), 38–41.

Elliot, E. J. (1997). Standards project emphasizes performance assessment. *NCATE Quality: The Newsletter of the National Council for Accreditation of Teacher Education, 6*(2), 6–8.

Farr, R., & Tone, B. (1994). *Portfolio and performance assessment.* Fort Worth, TX: Harcourt Brace College Publishers.

Ford, M. P., & Ohlhausen, M. M. (1991, December). Portfolio assessment in teacher education courses: Impact on students' beliefs, attitudes and habits. Paper presented at the 41st annual meeting of the National Reading Conference, Palm Springs, CA.

Gardner, H. (1991). *The unschooled mind: How children think and how schools should teach.* New York: Basic Books.

McTighe, J. (1996–1997). What happens between assessments? *Educational Leadership, 54*(4), 6–12.

Meisels, S . (1996–1997). Using work sampling in authentic assessments. *Educational Leadership, 54*(4), 60–65.

Meyer, C. (1992). What's the difference between authentic and performance assessment? *Educational Leadership, 49*(8), 39–40.

Mokhtari, K., Yellin, D., Bull, K., & Montgomery, D. (1996). Portfolio assessment in teacher education: Impact on preservice teachers' knowledge and attitudes. *Journal of Teacher Education, 47*(4), 245–252.

National Board for Professional Teaching Standards. (1991). *Toward high and rigorous standards for the teaching profession* (3rd ed.). Detroit, MI: Author.

National Commission on Teaching and America's Future. (1996). *What matters most: Teaching for America's future.* New York: Author.

Newmann, F., & Wehlage, G. (1993). Five standards of authentic instruction. *Educational Leadership, 50*(7), 8–12.

Nordquist, G. (1993). Japanese education: No recipe for authentic learning. *Educational Leadership. 50*(7), 64–67.

Schickendanz, J., York, M., Stewart, I., & White, D. (1990). *Strategies for teaching young children* (3rd ed.). Englewood, NJ: Prentice-Hall.

Suchman, J. R. (1964). Studies in inquiry training. In R. Ripple & V. Bookcastle (Eds.), *Piaget reconsidered.* Ithaca, NY: Cornell University.

Van Wagenen, L., & Hibbard, K. M. (1998). Building teacher portfolios. *Educational Leadership, 56*(5), 26–29.

Wiggins, G. (1992). Creating tests worth taking. *Educational Leadership, 49*(8), 26–33.

Wiggins, G. (1996–1997). Practicing what we preach in designing authentic assessments. *Educational Leadership, 54*(4), 18–25.

Wise, A. E. (1998). NCATE 2000 will emphasize candidate performance. *NCATE Quality: The Newsletter of the National Council for Accreditation of Teacher Education, 7*(2), 61–62.

Wolf, K. (1996). Developing an effective teaching portfolio. *Educational Leadership, 53*(6), 34–37.

NOTES

NOTES

NOTES

NOTES

NOTES

NOTES